P9-DGM-212

INSIGHT ⊙ GUIDES

EXPLORE

BUDAPEST

PLAN & BOOK
YOUR TAILOR-MADE TRIP

BRAZIL CHILE ECUADOR

TAILOR-MADE TRIPS & UNIQUE EXPERIENCES CREATED BY LOCAL TRAVEL EXPERTS AT INSIGHTGUIDES.COM/HOLIDAYS

Insight Guides has been inspiring travellers with high-quality travel content for over 45 years. As well as our popular guidebooks, we now offer the opportunity to book tailor-made private trips completely personalised to your needs and interests. By connecting with one of our local experts, you will directly benefit from their expertise and local know-how, helping you create memories that will last a lifetime.

HOW INSIGHTGUIDES.COM/HOLIDAYS WORKS

STEP 1

Pick your dream destination and submit an enquiry, or modify an existing itinerary if you prefer.

STEP 2

Fill in a short form, sharing details of your travel plans and preferences with a local expert.

STEP 3

Your local expert will create your personalised itinerary, which you can amend until you are completely satisfied.

STEP 4

Book securely online. Pack your bags and enjoy your holiday! Your local expert will be available to answer questions during your trip.

BENEFITS OF PLANNING & BOOKING AT
INSIGHTGUIDES.COM/HOLIDAYS

PLANNED BY LOCAL EXPERTS
The Insight Guides local experts are hand-picked, based on their experience in the travel industry and their impeccable standards of customer service.

SAVE TIME & MONEY
When a local expert plans your trip, you save time and money when you book, even during high season. You won't be charged for using a credit card either.

TAILOR-MADE TRIPS
Book with Insight Guides, and you will be in complete control of the planning process, from the initial selections to amending your final itinerary.

BOOK & TRAVEL STRESS-FREE
Enjoy stress-free travel when you use the Insight Guides secure online booking platform. All bookings come with a money-back guarantee.

WHAT OTHER TRAVELLERS THINK ABOUT TRIPS BOOKED
AT INSIGHTGUIDES.COM/HOLIDAYS

Trip to Portugal

Every step of the planning process and the trip itself was effortless and exceptional. Our special interests, preferences and requests were accommodated resulting in a trip that exceeded our expectations.

Corinne, USA   ★★★★★

Trip to Vietnam

The organization was superb, the drivers professional, and accommodation quite comfortable. I was well taken care of! My thanks to your colleagues who helped make my trip to Vietnam such a great experience.

Heather   ★★★★★

DON'T MISS OUT
BOOK NOW AT
INSIGHTGUIDES.COM/HOLIDAYS

CONTENTS

ARCHITECTURE BUFFS

Miklós Ybl's buildings, like the Hungarian State Opera (route 4) and those in the Palace District (route 6), capture Budapest's golden age, while Ödön Lechner's Royal Postal Savings Bank showcases the exquisite local Art Nouveau style (route 2).

RECOMMENDED ROUTES FOR...

BARS AND NIGHTLIFE

Stop by Szimpla Kert, Budapest's first and most famous ruin bar (route 3), before heading over to the IX District to experience the craft-beer scene (route 8).

FAMILIES

Children can make friends at the Budapest Zoo (route 5), ride the Children's Railway up in the Buda Hills (route 10) or enjoy a family picnic on Margaret Island (route 7).

FOODIES

Learn all about Hungarian produce at the Great Market Hall (route 8), dine at Michelin-starred Onyx (route 2) or pay a visit to Gundel, the home of Hungarian cooking (route 5).

HIKERS

The Buda Hills offer a mixture of pretty villas and scenic woodland (route 10). For a trek closer to town, ascend Gellért Hill for views over the Danube (route 9).

HISTORY LOVERS

Wander the historic streets around the Royal Palace (route 1), discover the old Jewish ghetto in the heart of the city (route 3) or the medieval ruins on Margaret Island (route 7).

OFF THE BEATEN TRACK

Recent renovation works have turned the former industrial IX District into a lively cultural hub (route 8). Come here or venture into the Buda Hills (route 10) to escape the crowds.

SHOPAHOLICS

You'll find all the top names on Andrássy Avenue (route 4) or Váci utca (route 2), but for quirky, Hungarian design head to Király utca (route 3) or Bartók Béla út (route 9).

INTRODUCTION

An introduction to Budapest's geography, customs and culture, plus illuminating background information on cuisine, history and what to do when you're there.

South Pest's Great Market Hall

EXPLORE BUDAPEST

Split in two by the Danube River, Budapest is famous for its impressive Royal Palace, its octet of bridges, thermal baths and ruin pubs. Hungary's capital is one of Europe's most beautiful cities, with a colourful history and a thriving cultural scene.

Budapest lies in the central-northern part of Hungary, towards the Slovakian border and just a few hours' train ride away from both Vienna and Bratislava. Its name derives from two historically independent cities on either side of the Danube: Buda and Pest.

To the west of the city, Buda's hilly topography is punctuated with medieval streets, Ottoman relics and grand villas, and you'll even find Roman ruins in the district known as Óbuda. In contrast, Pest – to the east – stretches out along a flat terrain that marks the beginning of the Great Hungarian Plain, set with grand tree-lined boulevards and imposing architecture.

In 1873, the three cities of Buda, Pest and Óbuda unified to become one city. Lying at the heart of Central Europe, Budapest is no stranger to attack, from the 1241–2 Mongol invasion to its 150-year-occupation by the Ottomans before falling under Habsburg rule. On top of this, Budapest still bears the scars from two world wars and the 1956 uprising against the Soviet forces.

As a destination, Budapest has a lot to offer. Firstly, it's a spa city, so you can take to the waters and luxuriate in won-derfully decadent surroundings. It is also a city of culture. The banks of the Danube and the Castle District of Buda, as well as Andrássy Avenue and the surrounding historical areas, are designated Unesco World Heritage Sites, and there are plenty of excellent museums and galleries to explore.

To top it all off, Hungarian cuisine has made great advances in recent decades, ushering in a new generation of chefs serving up innovative dishes and giving Hungarian classics a modern twist.

GEOGRAPHY AND LAYOUT

Budapest is divided into districts not dissimilar to Paris's arrondissements. There are 23 districts (*kerület*), identified by Roman numerals, that roughly spiral out from the Royal Palace in a clockwise direction. Most of Budapest's most famous sites lie within districts I, II, V, VI and VII, but travellers may head up to District XIV for City Park and its surroundings, and districts VIII, IX and even XI are gradually growing in popularity thanks to development initiatives.

Getting around Budapest is easy, either on foot or using the highly effi-

The colourful roof of Matthias Church

cient public-transport system. The network is made up of metro lines, tram lines and bus routes, as well as the public Danube boats, trolley buses and the cogwheel railway (see page 88). Areas of natural beauty such as the Buda Hills are easily accessible from Budapest, as are the towns and villages along the scenic Danube Bend.

HISTORY

The Carpathian and Danube basins have been inhabited since around 350,000 BC, but the first identified occupants were a Celtic-Illyrian people who established a tribal capital on top of Gellért Hill and a settlement in Óbuda.

From the 1st century AD, Roman legions advanced on the Danube, establishing a military camp called Aquincum on what was then the northern border of the Roman Empire, which grew into a populous city in its own right. Following the Romans, Attila the Hun arrived and captured the settlement, and the Huns occupied the area until the 9th century.

The Magyars date their arrival to around AD 890. This nomadic tribe are believed to originate from an area located between the Volga River and the Ural Mountains, and it was these people who gave the country its present name (*Magyarország* in Hungarian) and its language (*Magyar*).

The modern state of Hungary was established as a Christian one in 1000, when Magyar King István (who was later canonised) was crowned first king of Hungary. The new and stable country began to build itself up until the Mongol invasion in 1241–2 razed and devastated its capital; after their retreat, King Béla IV was left to restore the nation and rebuilt the city.

The 15th century saw a period of economic and cultural growth for both Hungary and Budapest, which flourished under the rule of King Mátyás Corvin (born Hunyadi). The country enjoyed a golden age of intellectual, artistic and civic development.

In 1490, Mátyás died without an heir, and a period of peasant rebellion and instability paved the way for the Turks to assimilate much of Hungary, including the capital, into the Ottoman Empire between 1541 and 1699.

Under Habsburg rule

In 1686–7, the Holy Alliance (comprising the Habsburgs, Poland and Venice) liberated Buda, incorporating Hungary into the Habsburg Empire. Many Hungarians, however, wanted independence. From 1703–11, Prince Ferenc Rákóczi (a descendant of the princes of Transylvania) became leader of the independence struggle. A peasant uprising soon turned into a battle for liberation, but the country was too ravaged by war and poverty to sustain a rebellion.

Peace lasted until 1848, when a group of young intellectuals, headed up by poet Sándor Petőfi, instigated another rebellion. Emperor Franz Josef I crushed the revolt the following year

All smiles at a Budapest café

after summoning help from the Tsar of Russia. But something had to be done, and the solution – the Compromise of 1867 – rebranded the Austrian Empire as the Austro-Hungarian Empire, with Franz Josef as dual monarch.

Until World War I, Budapest grew faster than any other city in Europe. Count István Széchenyi, who was a powerful force in the area's development, also sought to unite the towns of Buda, Óbuda and Pest into one city. Wedded in name and status in 1873, Széchenyi is also credited with responsibility for the Chain Bridge, which was the first permanent bridge linking the sides of the city.

World War I brought the golden age of the fin de siécle to an end. Austro-Hungary was defeated and the empire collapsed. Count Mihály Károlyi established an independent republic, but resigned in March 1919. After this, the Communist Party, led by Béla Kun, established a Soviet Republic. However, this was brought down shortly afterwards, when the country was occupied and looted by Romanian forces.

In 1920, Admiral Miklós Horthy was proclaimed regent. Although the country was a monarchy once again, it was decided not to recall the king.

World War II
An uneasy alliance with Germany existed throughout World War II, which ended in March 1944 when German troops occupied Hungary. However, the Soviet Army was advancing fast and the Germans were defeated after the Siege of Budapest. Budapest fell in February 1945, with three-quarters of its buildings destroyed and a death toll of half a million, and the Russians assumed control of the city.

Soviet rule and post-Soviet reality
In 1949, Hungary became the People's Republic under Soviet rule. After seven years of brutal repression, 50,000 students and workers marched on parliament to air their grievances on 23 October 1956. Soviet retribution only took 12 days and on 4 November, Red Army tanks rolled into Budapest and crushed the resistance. The West watched in horror as thousands were executed. Some 25,000 Hungarians died and 200,000 fled the country.

In 1988–9, with the effects of *glasnost* and *perestroika* being felt throughout the Eastern bloc, Hungary experienced many changes, culminating in the country holding its first free elections in 43 years in 1990. Restored to being a democratic republic, a conservative government was the first to take power. In 1991, the last Soviet soldier left, and Hungary became an associate member of the European Union (EU); in 1994, a reformed socialist party came to power and in 1999 Hungary joined NATO. On 1 May 2004, Hungary became a full EU member. The 2009 financial crisis, the rise of Viktor Orbán and the Fidesz party along with the refugee and migrant crisis have brought Hungary into political conflict with the EU

Elderly residents catching up

Playing chess at Széchenyi Baths

over a multitude of issues. The outcome of these disputes is still very much in flux.

CLIMATE

Hungary is a landlocked country in Central Europe. Budapest experiences continental weather patterns with cold winters that plunge into the minuses, sometimes with snow, and on rare occasions, ice on the Danube. In the summer, temperatures can be sweltering, punctuated by heavy showers and thunderstorms. Even if the summer promises dry heat, bring an umbrella just to be safe.

DON'T LEAVE BUDAPEST WITHOUT...

Taking a dip in one of the thermal baths. The city is famous for its thermal springs and exquisite thermal baths, from the 16th-century Ottoman hammams to the Belle Epoque beauties (see page 61).

Drinking in a ruin pub. Pay a visit to Szimpla Kert or another of Budapest's vibrant ruin bars for a beer (see pages 52 and 107). If you're feeling brave, try *pálinka*, the local fire water.

Boating on the Danube. Budapest's most beautiful views lie along the Danube, and what better way to see it than from the blue river itself. You can either book onto one of the sightseeing tour boats or catch the public boat in the summer months (run by the BKK, Budapest's official public-transport company).

Sampling some Hungarian food. From *gulyás* (goulash) to paprika chicken and street food like *lángos* (a deep-fried flatbread), make sure you don't leave Budapest without trying some Hungarian specialties (see page 16).

Exploring the Castle District. For architecture and history, the area around the Royal Palace is one of the richest in the city, with world-class views and sightseeing (see page 30).

Visiting a synagogue. Immerse yourself in Budapest's Jewish history by discovering one of the synagogues in the historic Jewish Quarter (see page 47).

Checking out some Hungarian design. Budapest was awarded the Unesco Creative Cities title for its design, so explore some of its collectives and boutiques for unique goodies to take home (see page 21).

Strolling Andrássy Avenue. Budapest's answer to the Champs Élyseés, this elegant boulevard stretches over 2km (1.5 miles) from St Stephen's Basilica to Heroes' Square – it's worth taking the time to explore it properly. You can also ride the Millennium Underground Railway, which is more than 100 years old and was the first metro line in continental Europe.

Going to a concert. Hungary is famous for its classical composers. With the Hungarian State Opera House, the Palace of Arts, the Liszt Ferenc Academy and St Stephen's Basilica – which organises organ concerts – you'll be spoilt for choice when deciding where to go and what to see.

POPULATION AND PEOPLE

Budapest is Hungary's largest city by far, home to a population of approximately 1.77 million – 18% of the country lives in the capital alone. While the majority of Budapest's demographic is Hungarian, you'll also find a large Roma minority, along with people from neighbouring countries, such as Romania, Slovakia, Germany and Serbia, and from further afield, such as China and Vietnam. The population is relatively young, especially with Budapest's dense concentration of universities, as well as those from smaller towns who move to the capital for work and the city lifestyle.

Following the Soviet period, Budapest has embraced consumer culture and Western brands, with around 20 modern shopping centres and numerous hypermarkets and fast-food outlets.

Hungarians are renowned for their friendliness. If they speak English (which many of them do – particularly the younger generations) and see you looking at a map, they will likely stop to help. If they don't speak English, they'll try their best anyway – confronted with a foreigner who has got lost, missed a bus stop or can't understand the transport ticket machine, Hungarians will often take it upon themselves to sort out the situation.

POLITICS AND ECONOMICS

On 1 May 2004 there were fireworks, celebrations and flag-waving as Hungary became a fully-fledged member of the EU, following a vote the previous year. The then Prime Minister, Péter Medgyessy, said 'We can't expect Europe to offer a miracle. The miracle isn't within Europe. The miracle is within us.' Certainly, the following years proved challenging.

Ineffective budgetary management made the country vulnerable to the world financial crisis of 2008, and to avoid the collapse of its currency, Hungary negotiated a US$25 billion bail-out with the IMF. The people signalled their frustration in the 2010 elections, replacing Socialists with Conservatives, and Fidesz leader, Viktor Orbán, took the office of prime minister. In the 2014 parliamentary elections, the ruling party won a sweeping victory, staying in power. Despite this, some

Liberty Monument

A nighttime view of Budapest

of the party motions – such as their 2016 (failed) anti-refugee bill and 2017 legislation thought to have targeted the Central European University – have invited criticism from world leaders and the international media.

TOP TIPS FOR VISITING BUDAPEST

Public transport. Budapest has a well-connected and efficient public-transport network that relies on a trust system. If you buy a single ticket, make sure you validate it before or as soon as you board. On the metro, do this before descending the escalators; on trams and buses, use the machine on board and keep the ticket. If you have a pass, keep it on you at all times. Random checks by ticket inspectors wearing a BKK armband and sometimes a uniform (but most often in plain clothes) occur frequently, and travelling without a valid ticket or a pass can result in heavy fines.

The currency. The currency in Hungary is the Hungarian forint. Prices and bank notes go up to the thousands (the highest note denomination is 20,000 Ft), so it can be hard to keep track of your spending. Check the exchange rate or use an app to calculate the amount so you don't overpay or get taken advantage of.

Places of worship. Most religious monuments don't have a specific dress code, although men will have to wear a *kippah* or a *yamaka* in the synagogues, and women should cover their arms going into both churches and synagogues.

Souvenirs. Pick up something unique and Hungarian for your friends and family back home. Opt for a bag of paprika, Hungarian wine or some embroidery, or get a more contemporary item from a Hungarian designer.

Hiking. Budapest has several excellent scenic trails going up into the hills, so bring some hiking shoes with you. Make sure to wear socks and invest in a good bug spray, as ticks can be a risk in the wooded areas of the city suburbs in the warmer months.

Taxis. Only book a taxi through one of the official companies; Budapest Taxi and FőTaxi are two of the best, or you can use an app like Bolt (formerly known as Taxify). Never flag down a taxi on the street, as there are many cowboy taxis in Budapest looking to take advantage of foreign visitors.

Tipping. While not mandatory in Hungary, tipping is encouraged. Hungarians usually round up the bill when paying and give a total amount rather than leave coins on the table. A 10 percent tip is acceptable. If you hand over a large note saying 'thank you', the server may assume you're including the tip and you may not get any change back.

Bath etiquette. Bring some shower slippers and your own towel when visiting the baths (you can rent towels, but it's probably more comfortable to use your own). Unless you're visiting a single-sex bath (like Rudas on the weekdays), you must wear swimwear. If you're planning on using the swimming pools, make sure you take a swimming cap or a shower cap to cover your hair.

Grilled perch

FOOD AND DRINK

Hungarian food tends to be hearty, often featuring meat, potatoes and pickles accented with liberal doses of sweet and spicy paprika, which is then washed down with local wine and rounded off with a shot of pálinka or bitter Unicum.

Magyar cuisine has a long history, but is little known outside Hungary. Traditionally, the nomadic Magyars cooked their food in a cast-iron cauldron called a *bogrács* over an open fire, and traces of this kind of one-pot cooking can still be found in the hearty soups and cabbage-based dishes that crop up on many menus today. In the 17th century, paprika arrived in the country. Some say the Slavs or the Turks brought it, others say it came from the Americas. Paprika is a relatively mild seasoning, which should not be confused with the far hotter chilli; although that doesn't mean hot and spicy varieties don't exist. Hungarian food is generally cooked in lard or goose fat, which lends it a heavier consistency and a richer taste than many Westerners are accustomed to. If restaurant portions are too hefty, order soup and then an appetiser instead of a main course. Some restaurants also offer smaller portions.

Budapest has not always been known for its adventurous cooking, but things are starting to change. There are chefs working in the city today who have brought an innovative 21st-century touch to old recipes, making them far more inviting. You'll find contemporary interpretations of Hungarian cuisine, from pop-up restaurants giving you a true taste of home cooking to Michelin-starred takes on classic Magyar dishes, as well as trendy Hungarian street food. Molecular gastronomy dishes – such as pickles frozen in liquid nitrogen – may even make it onto the menu. There are also an increasing number of vegan and vegetarian options.

LOCAL CUISINE

While Hungarian cuisine is largely seasonal – with cold fruit soups or *lecsó*, a Hungarian ratatouille, in the summer, goose specials in November and stuffed cabbage (*töltött káposzta*) filled with meat around Christmas and New Year – you'll find the usual suspects on the menu all year round.

Classic Hungarian dishes include the eponymous goulash soup (*gulyásleves*), which contrary to popular belief is a soup and not a stew, made with chunks of beef, potatoes, onions, peppers, tomatoes and, of course, seasoned with liberal quantities of

Modern Hungarian dish

The ubiquitous beef stew with dumplings

paprika, and paprika chicken (*paprikás csirke*), a dish made using chicken legs or thighs, cooked in a sauce consisting of paprika, green peppers, onions and sour cream, which is usually served with a gnocchi-like dumpling called *galuska* or *nokedli*.

Soups are a staple in the Hungarian kitchen, and beyond the goulash, you also have fishermen's soup, which has a similar base but uses pieces of fresh-water fish instead of meat, and a lighter consommé called *erőleves*, usually served with an egg yolk.

Mains usually involve a piece of meat, usually veal or pork, fried, breaded and served with potatoes and sour pickles or sauerkraut. Meat stews, called *pörkölt*, are also popular, and usually come with a choice of meats, from beef (*mar-hapörkölt*) to venison (*vadaspörkölt*). Game is popular in Hungary, and won't break the bank, especially if you order venison or wild boar.

While vegetarian dishes seem few and far between, you will find fried cheese *(rántott sajt)* or fried and stuffed mushrooms *(rántott gomba)*. You may discover a Caesar or Greek salad in select restaurants, but *saláta* usually means a plate of cabbage and pickled beetroot; what most Western-ers call a mixed salad usually appears as *vitamin saláta*. Strict vegetarians will need to monitor the menu closely: classic dishes of stuffed pepper *(töltött paprika)* and stuffed cabbage *(töltött káposzta)* actually include pork in the filling, and while *lecsó*, a stew made from peppers, tomatoes and onions, seems veggie friendly, it may have been cooked with lard, not to mention many vegetable soups include some meat or meat stock.

When it comes to desserts, Hungar-ians love pastries and sweets. Try the Gundel pancake (*palacsinta*), named after Hungary's most famous restau-rateur, which comes filled with nut and raisin paste, drenched in chocolate and rum sauce and sometimes flambéed. Another classic you should try is *som-lói galuska*, a heavy sponge with vanilla, nuts, chocolate and whipped cream in an orange and rum sauce. Strudels (*rétes*) often have fruit, sweetened cot-tage cheese and poppy-seed fillings.

WHERE TO EAT

You won't often see the sign 'restau-rant' in Budapest; when you do, the establishment is likely to cater to for-eign tourists. The two most common names for a place to eat are *étterem* and *vendéglő*. A *csárda* (pronounced chard-a) is usually a country-style inn with a cosy atmosphere. Budapest has long rivalled Vienna for its café culture and love of pastries and coffee. Many cafés (*kávéház* and *cukrászda*) serve full meals as well as cakes.

Breakfast *(reggeli)* is generally served from 7–10am. Hungarians don't eat much at the start of the day, but at most hotels a basic interna-

Make sure to try Budapest's street food

tional breakfast buffet is served. Lunch *(ebéd)*, generally served from 1–3pm, is the main meal of the day, a fact reflected in the quantities that tend to appear. Dinner *(vacsora)* is served from 7–10pm, although Hungarians in general are not late eaters.

LOCAL DRINKS

Over the last decade or so, Hungary has slowly been getting recognition for its wines. Throughout the country you'll find a variety of wines grown in different regions, from the sweet dessert wines from Tokaj to the dry, spicy reds from Villány.

The most famous of Hungary's white wines is Tokaj, a rich, aged dessert wine that has been produced for more than 200 years. It has long been a favourite of monarchs, such as Catherine the Great and Louis XIV. The grapes that produce this celebrated variety are grown in the volcanic soil of the Tokaj region in the northeast of Hungary. The grapes are left on the vine until autumn mists encourage the growth of the noble rot that gives the wine its intense sweetness and complex character. However, you can also find excellent dry whites from this region, such as Tokaji Furmint. Tokaji Szamorodni is medium-sweet, akin to sherry, and Tokaji Aszú is full-bodied and sweet.

The Villány region produces some of Hungary's best reds, many of which are aged in oak casks, including the fine Villányi Burgundi and the tannic Kékoportó. The best-known Hungarian red, which comes from the northeastern region, is the splendidly named 'Bull's Blood of Eger' (Egri Bikavér) – a full-bodied and spicy accompaniment to meat or game dishes. More subtle is the Pinot Noir from the same town.

Less distinguished but perfectly satisfying white table wines come from the Lake Balaton region, including Riesling, Sauvignon Blanc and Chardonnay. Badacsonyi wines are the best known and have been enjoyed for some 2,000 years. Some of the best white wines

Street food

Over the past few years, street food has become increasingly popular in Budapest, with food trucks, gourmet street food restaurants and food courts popping up all over the city. While you'll find the usual burgers, chips and pizzas on offer, you can also try some more local dishes. The most popular is *lángos*, a deep-fried dough that's usually topped with sour cream and cheese. You can also sample Hungarian sausage dishes, modern street food takes on the classic fried cheese and Hungarian-Jewish street food. If you've got a sweet tooth, choose one of the famous chimney cakes *(kürtöskalács)*, a sweet brioche-like pastry baked over charcoal and rolled in cinnamon, cocoa powder, ground walnuts and more.

Cake slices are aplenty in Budapest

in the country come from the smallest wine-producing region, Somló.

In the summer, Hungarians drink *fröccs*, a white wine or rosé spritzer that comes in varying ratios – perfect for the heat.

Budapest also produces its own sparkling wine, the most famous being from Törley, whose labyrinthine cellars are located in the suburbs of the city in Budafok. Its grapes come from nearby Etyek – said to have a climate similar to that of Champagne. While most bottles are produced using the Charmant technique, you can find a bottle of Törley that's a Brut Nature or fermented in the bottle.

While Hungary's wine has been gaining international recognition, its craft-beer scene has also been brewing. Today, there are over 70 breweries in the country, offering alternatives to the usual Hungarian factory beers like Soproni, Dreher and Borsodi. Small breweries like Hübris, Mad Scientist and Távoli Galaxis, among others, have revolutionised the Hungarian beer scene, turning it into more than just an accompaniment to the heavy and spicy Hungarian food.

Beyond the beer and wine scene, other local drinks include Hungary's famous fruit brandies *(pálinka)*. This powerful firewater is made from fermented, local fruit before being distilled and aged in the bottle. You can find varieties in pear *(körte)*, plum *(szilva)*, apricot *(barack)*, cherry *(cseresznye)*, apple *(alma)* and even more variations. It's often drunk as a digestive, but some say it also opens the stomach up for food as an apéritif.

And finally, the country's national drink – the bitter green herbal liqueur that comes in an orb-shaped bottle – the iconic Zwack Unicum. The concoction is more than 200 years old and is made from 40 herbs and spices, and its recipe is a closely guarded family secret.

Coffee *(kávé)* is commonly served black, hot and sweet, espresso-style in thimble-sized cups. There used to be no alternative, but now you'll find milk available everywhere, and cappuccinos are served all over Budapest and other large towns. The capital has also seen a renaissance in third-wave coffee shops, so you can get your pour overs, lattes and flat whites in some of the city's more trendy modern cafés. Some of the newer coffee houses also work with local roasters.

Tea is also widely available, and a request for Earl Grey, or any other familiar type, with lemon or milk, will raise no eyebrows in decent coffee houses.

Food and Drink Prices

Price guide for a two-course meal for one with a glass of house wine:

€€€€ = over 60 euros
€€€ = 40–60 euros
€€ = 20–40 euros
€ = below 20 euros

Budapest fridge magnets

SHOPPING

Shopping in Budapest means more than going home with colourful bags of paprika and embroidered tablecloths. Bring back a bottle of Hungarian wine, a piece of unique, local design or even an antique sourced from a flea market.

SHOPPING AREAS

Budapest is no longer the bargain retail experience it once was, and prices for many goods are about the same as those in other European capitals. Shopping has undergone a revolution in Budapest in recent years, and the results are that you'll find a diverse range of items sold across the city.

When it comes to shopping in Budapest, it's useful to know exactly what it is you want to buy. Whether you're looking to take home the usual souvenirs or to pick up something a bit different, it's important to head for the right district — from the souvenir shops of V District to the design stores of the Jewish Quarter and the foodie goods on offer at South Pest's Great Market Hall.

Central Budapest: V District
If the regular souvenir shops make it easier to buy goodies for loved ones back home, then Váci utca (see page 44) comes densely packed with them. You'll find postcards, magnets, Budapest themed T-shirts, aprons and more along this central shopping street.

For something more upmarket, head to the shops around Deák Ferenc utca, also dubbed 'Fashion Street', which offers a mix of international fashion brands.

Located on the fringes of the V District, close to Margaret Bridge (see page 75), Falk Miksa utca is a hub of antique shops and fine art galleries. If you're armed with a generous shopping budget, take home an antique or a painting from one of the galleries or antiquarians found along this street.

The Jewish Quarter: VII District
The Jewish Quarter (see page 46) is a hub of quirky and hipster design stores. On the weekends, check out the market at Gozsdú udvar, which boasts a combination of antiques, vintage memorabilia and stalls featuring local designers. Sunday morning is a good time to do some shopping in the area, as ruin pub Szimpla Kert hosts a lively farmers' market, where you can find produce ranging from cheeses to honey and jam.

If you head over to the Klauzál tér market hall, there is also an antiques market — Antik Placc — in full swing. Most of the objects here have been renovated, redesigned and modified to cre-

Embroidery for sale   *Much of the local porcelain is exquisite*

ate completely unique items that keep the charm of their originals, while also capturing new trends.

South Pest: IX District and beyond

For food and souvenirs, the Great Market Hall (see page 77) is the ideal spot. You can source a variety of ingredients, such as wine, paprika, Hungarian cured meats and other local specialties. On the first floor, you'll also find folk crafts, such as embroidery, lace, carved items and more. Close to the market, the Whale (Bálna) is also a venue for antique and design shopping (see page 78). If you're serious about picking up curiosities, take the 54 or 55 bus from Boráros tér to the Ecseri Market, a large outdoor market specialising in antiques, retro items and other odd bits.

WHAT TO BUY

Folk art and crafts. Hungary has a rich heritage when it comes to folk art and crafts. One of the most notable – and more easily portable – gifts is an embroidered tablecloth or a shirt decorated with colourful floral patterns. Hungary is known for its embroidered textiles, with the best-known varieties coming from Kalocsa, Mezőkovesd and Kalotaszeg, although you can find all kinds in Budapest. Leatherwork and elaborately carved wood or copper items are also available in any souvenir shop, market or traditional crafts shop.

Wine and pálinka. With Hungarian wine on the rise, you can't go wrong with a bottle of Tokaj. This amber-coloured dessert wine is professed to be the 'Wine of Kings' for its popularity with royals throughout history. However, a bottle of good Hungarian red, like a spicy wine from Szekszárd or Villány, also makes a good souvenir. For something a bit stronger, take home a bottle of quality *pálinka*. You can get aged *pálinka* for that more traditional, matured, classic brandy taste.

Paprika. Hungary and paprika go hand in hand, and the best paprika comes from the southern city of Szeged. You can get different types of ground paprika powder ranging in potency from sweet variety (*csemege*) to hot (*erős*), which also ranges from mildly hot to very spicy.

Local design. Budapest has been awarded the Unesco City of Culture for its design, so peruse some of the smaller boutiques, or the hidden showrooms in courtyards or tucked up in private apartments. These invariably feature young Hungarian designers, with goods ranging from clothing to shoes and accessories.

Porcelain. Herend and Zsolnay earned their reputation around the world for their glazed vases and ceramics. Keep an eye out for their shops and showrooms around the city centre, or see if you can find any original antiques from these world-class porcelain factories in the city's higher-end antique shops.

Sziget Festival

ENTERTAINMENT

Whether you want to see a classical concert, spend an evening at the opera or hit the ruin bars, Budapest has enough quality entertainment to cater to everyone's taste, whims and wallet.

You'll always find something going on in the Hungarian capital. Keep an eye out for pop-up events, as there are a number of outdoor culinary and cultural festivals taking place throughout the year in the city's public spaces. But beyond that, Budapest has a full programme of events gracing its auditoriums and quirky smaller venues, not to mention behind the crumbling walls of its ruin pubs and basement bars.

Ruin pubs

In the early 2000s, many buildings in the Jewish Quarter were left in a neglected state and practically abandoned. In 2002, Ábel Zsendovits and friends opened up Szimpla, initially on Kertész utca, where you'll find the Szimpla Café today. Then, in 2004, the Szimpla crew took a gamble on a condemned building on Kazinczy utca and created the first ruin bar. This use of an abandoned space brought in the young and creative crowds, and soon other so-called ruin bars popped up all over the city, mainly in the VII District. A ruin bar usually comes with the following characteristics: a crumbling building, eclectic, mismatched furniture and quirky art.

THEATRE AND DANCE

Hungarians love theatre, which is why you'll find the city's own 'Budapest Broadway' on Nagymező utca (see page 56), with venues such as the Hungarian Operetta Theatre, Thália Theatre and Radnóti Theatre. Further up on Andrássy Avenue is Central Europe's largest Puppet Theatre.

If you head out to the Millennium Quarter, the National Theatre puts on some of the most cutting-edge theatre and dance productions in the country. However, finding English-language theatre in Budapest can be a real challenge, although smaller venues occasionally put on English-language productions from small collectives.

As an alternative, dance – from ballet to modern – is big in the city. You can take in a classical ballet (or opera production) at the Hungarian State Opera or the Erkel Theatre. Or, for something more avant-garde, try the dance productions at the Trafó House of Contemporary Arts.

MUSIC

Home to composers such as Liszt, Bartók and Kodály, Hungary has an

Uránia art–house cinema

Orchestral performance in the city

impressive pedigree when it comes to classical music. The best place to see big orchestras, from international ensembles to home-grown talent, is at the Palace of Arts, but you can also attend concerts inside the stunning fresco-studded Ferenc Liszt Music Academy (see page 56).

For something more modern, venues such as subterranean Akvárium Klub on Deák Ferenc tér and – in the summer – open-air Budapest Park and Barba Negra Track host big names from home and abroad. But it's the Sziget Festival (www.szigetfestival.com) in August that pulls in the crowds. In the middle of the month, Óbuda Island transforms into the 'Island of Freedom' for a weeklong music festival with both international and local performers.

You'll also find smaller, more alternative venues scattered throughout the city. One of these is A38, a former Ukrainian stone-carrying ship that is permanently moored along the Danube, which hosts concerts from a range of indie artists from Hungary and beyond.

FILM

Budapest has become a Hollywood hub over the past few decades, and it's likely you'll spot a street or two closed off for shooting while you're wandering around the city. From *Evita* to *Inferno*, Budapest has featured as a filming location. And Hungary is no shy candidate in the film industry, with László

Nemes' *Son of Saul* winning an Academy Award for Best Foreign Language Film in 2016 and Ildikó Enyedi's On Body and Soul nominated for the same award two years later.

The Hungarian capital hosts some unique and beautiful cinemas. The neo-Orientalist Uránia art-house cinema is one of Budapest's hidden treasures. Like Uránia, nearby gold-gilded Puskin, Gaudí-esque Művész and hipster-favourite Toldi all show films from across the world, and in the case of Toldi and Művész, even with English subtitles.

Some of the bigger Cineplexes will, like the beautiful neoclassical Corvin cinema, or the Cinema City in the Allée mall, show blockbusters with subtitles.

NIGHTLIFE

From its iconic ruin pubs to hip clubs and rooftop bars, Budapest has a vibrant nightlife that is very bar centric. Much of the action is centred around the Jewish Quarter, but the Inner City in the V District, with clubs like Ötkert, also draws the crowds. On Andrássy, Hello Baby is perhaps the largest, located in the courtyard of an old palatial building.

Grungy contender, Corvintető, is unique for being located on top of a Socialist Realist shopping centre, and hosts all-night parties with music ranging from techno to hip-hop. True techno lovers should head over to LÄRM, inside the Fogasház super ruin disco club.

Rudas Baths

THERMAL BATHS

Even before the Romans arrived, Budapest's thermal waters were recognised for their healing properties, fed by more than one hundred geothermal springs coursing beneath the city.

Budapest lies on a geological fault line marked by the Danube River; one side of the city lies on a flat plain, the other side rises up into hilly terrain. The baths in Budapest exist thanks to the fault line, and the fact that the Earth's crust is relatively thin around the Carpathian Basin: mineral waters are propelled up through the geological fault and can rise easily to the surface.

Budapest's bathing legacy has left the city with nine thermal baths and numerous outdoor thermal pools. Those constructed by the Turks during the Ottoman occupation of Buda date as far back as the 16th century. Budapest also saw a boom in bathing culture in the late-19th and early-20th centuries, when it built grand baths like the Széchenyi, turning the capital into a fin de siècle health resort.

Each spring comes with its own mineral content, and each bath is said to aid certain ailments – from arthritis and rheumatism to discus hernia and spinal deformity – by either bathing in the water or drinking it. In fact, some doctors prescribe the baths to their patients. Next to the main baths, you'll still find drinking halls where you can imbibe the water fresh from the source.

Széchenyi Baths. Among the grandest of Budapest's thermal baths, Széchenyi – unlike most of the city's baths – lies on the Pest side of the river. The water is sourced from an underground well, and is heated to varying temperatures to give each bath its desired properties. This grand neo-Baroque bath is one of the largest bath complexes in Central Europe, and arguably Budapest's most famous. On the weekends it hosts hedonistic 'Sparties', late night spa parties with DJs, lights and poolside bars.

Rudas Baths. The most famous of Budapest's Turkish Baths, the old part of the Rudas Thermal Bath was built in the 16th century. It's popular for its atmospheric feel, and offers a taste of the Turkish art of bathing. Sunlight filters in through holes in the 10-metre (33ft) cupola covering the central octagonal pool. This complex has been restored and expanded in recent years, and is popular for its rooftop Jacuzzi and sun terrace.

Gellért Baths. While Budapest's thermal waters are said to have curative properties, the architectural opulence of baths like the Gellért Thermal Baths attract the

A steamy 'Sparty' at Széchenyi

crowds. Accented with Zsolnay porcelain tiles and colonnaded pools, topped off with stained-glass ceilings, this bath has evolved considerably since its early days as a mud bath said to have 'miraculous' properties. In the early 20th century, the Gellért's outdoor pools were also home to one of the world's first wave machines, which made its debut in 1927.

Lukács Baths. The Lukács takes its water from the nearby Molnár János Cave, a 7km (4.3-mile) -long underground cavern filled with thermal waters rich in mineral deposits. While the Lukács may not boast the grandeur of its contemporaries such as the Széchenyi and the Gellért, nor have the historic appeal of the Ottoman baths, it's a firm favourite with the locals. Upon entering the courtyard, marble placards from grateful patients line the wall, thanking the baths for curing them. In the winter months, the Lukács take over from the Széchenyi with their 'Magic Spa Parties', held in the heated outdoor pools.

Király Baths. These are the oldest of the Turkish baths, and while the Király doesn't dazzle quite like the Rudas, the dilapidated state of these baths gives them their own antique charm. Built in 1565 by Arslan, the Pasha of Buda, and completed by his successor, Sokoli Mustafa, this bath actually has no direct access to a thermal spring. Since the Turks built the baths far from the source should the castle ever become besieged, it gets its water from today's Lukács Baths. The König

family (who gave the baths their current Hungarian name; *Király* meaning 'King') acquired the baths in 1796. The complex was damaged during World War II, and was last renovated in 1950. Unlike the Rudas Baths, which are single sex on weekdays, the Király Baths are co-ed all week long. A full renovation is scheduled which is set to last until 2020.

Veli Bej Baths. Hidden in a hospital next to the Lukács Baths, the Veli Bej Baths offer bathers the Ottoman experience, but with a cleaner, newer feel. These historic Turkish baths have been renovated and close at lunchtime. Since the number of bathers is capped, it's a good one to go to when you want to avoid the crowds.

Spas

You don't have to be suffering from a particular ailment to benefit from spa treatments, and there's nothing wrong with a little pampering when you are on holiday. In Hungary, health and wellness hotels and centres are major attractions, as well as the traditional thermal baths. These centres provide saunas and steam baths, therapy and relaxation, new-age treatments and alternative therapies, sport and exercise, gastronomy and a staggering number of beauty and style treatments. Even shopping malls have wellness and beauty centres: you can emerge detoxified, mentally alert and looking good.

Budapest in 1617

HISTORY: KEY DATES

From the Romans to the Magyars, through Ottoman and Habsburg empires, two world wars and decades of communism, Budapest is a city with a complex history that's as varied as the architecture left behind.

EARLY HISTORY

1st century AD Roman legions advance to the Danube.
890s The Magyars arrive in the area.
1000 Coronation of King István.
1222 Proclamation of the Golden Bull, Hungary's Magna Carta.
1241–2 Mongol invasion; famine and epidemics rife.
1301 Foundation of the Angevin dynasty by Károly Róbert.

RENAISSANCE HUNGARY AND THE OTTOMAN OCCUPATION

1444 János Hunyadi chosen as regent.
1456 Hunyadi's victory over the Ottomans at Nándorfehérvár (Belgrade).
1526 Battle of Móhacs divides Hungary and ushers in Ottoman rule, which lasts 150 years.

HABSBURG EMPIRE

1686–7 Liberation of Budapest by the Holy Alliance.
1703–11 Unsuccessful independence struggle led by Ferenc Rákóczi.
1848–9 Rebellion of intellectuals, led by Sándor Petőfi.
1867 Foundation of the Austro-Hungarian Empire.
1873 Budapest formed from Buda, Pest and Óbuda.

EARLY 20TH CENTURY

1918 Austro-Hungarian Empire falls apart after World War I, and the Hungarian republic is proclaimed.
1919 Communists take power, led by Béla Kun, who wages war on Czechoslovakia and Romania. Romanian forces occupy the Hungarian capital and power is passed to Miklós Horthy.
1920 Hungary is carved into pieces under the Treaty of Trianon, leaving a third of Hungarian native speakers residing outside the country.

Crowds take to Budapest's streets to proclaim the Republic of Hungary, 23 October 1989

1920 The Kingdom of Hungary is re-established and Admiral Horthy is made regent.

1938 Czechoslovakia cedes territory to Germany and Hungary regains some of its lost land.

1939 Hungary withdraws from the League of Nations after joining Anti-Comintern Pact of Germany, Japan and Italy. World War II breaks out.

1940 Hungary regains northern Transylvania from Romania.

1941 German invasion of the Soviet Union. The Hungarian army, allied with Germany, suffers huge losses on the Eastern Front.

1944 Hungary falls to German forces and Hungarian Nazis seize power following Horthy's request to advancing Soviets for an armistice.

COMMUNIST RULE

1945 Soviet Army defeats Germans and repressive Soviet rule ensues.

1956 The Hungarian revolution is brutally crushed by the Soviet Union. Communist Party leader János Kádár is installed in power.

1958 Imre Nagy, prime minister during the 1956 revolt, is executed.

1988–9 The Communist Party responds to public dissatisfaction as Soviet leader Gorbachev promises no more interference in Hungarian affairs.

POST-COMMUNIST HUNGARY

1989 Republic of Hungary proclaimed.

1990 Free elections return the Conservative Democratic Forum.

1991 Last Soviet soldier departs from Hungarian soil.

2004 Hungary joins the EU.

2006 Riots follow Prime Minister Gyurcsany's admission of lying.

2008 Financial crisis forces Hungary to accept US$25.1bn rescue deal.

2010 Economic woes bring electoral disaster for the Socialist Party.

2014 Ruling party Fidesz, led by Viktor Orbán, wins parliamentary elections.

2015 Migrant crisis hits Hungary.

2016 Hundreds of people rally in Budapest against proposed anti-terror measures.

2017 The Hungarian government attempts to shut down the liberal Central European University. The European Parliament threatens to suspend Hungary from the EU.

2018 Victor Orbán and his Fidesz party win a third term in office.

2019 A sightseeing boat sinks in the River Danube. Almost 30 people die.

2020 Three stages of the Giro d'Italia are scheduled in Hungary.

2021 The UEFA European Under-21 Championship is set to take place in Hungary and Slovenia.

BEST ROUTES

CASTLE HILL

Set atop a rocky plateau overlooking the Danube, Castle Hill is a historical tapestry. Thirteenth-century ruins and grand Habsburg monuments are interlaced with winding streets, museums, galleries and a hidden underground labyrinth of caves and subterranean passages.

DISTANCE: 3.5km (2.2 miles)
TIME: A full day
START: Chain Bridge
END: Vienna Gate
POINTS TO NOTE: If you're planning to visit any of the museums, avoid doing this walk on a Monday, as most of the museums and galleries close for the day.

King Béla IV established the Castle District in Buda during the late 13th century, after Mongol attacks ravaged the city. Over the centuries, despite its strategic location, the castle and surrounding district has been destroyed and rebuilt several times over. While much of the architecture today is Baroque, you'll still find echoes of the Renaissance citadel constructed during the reign of King Mátyás, along with relics left behind by the Ottoman Pashas. During World War II, much of the city – Castle Hill not excluded – was destroyed during the Siege of Budapest in 1945, in which the Germans held out here for

three months. Shelling devastated both the area around the Royal Palace and a substantial part of the Old Town, which has since been restored to much of its former glory.

Today, the winding pedestrian-friendly streets, lined with colourful Baroque houses and photogenic lookout points across the Danube to Pest, give this historic district a romantic feel.

ADAM CLARK SQUARE AND THE CHAIN BRIDGE

Begin at the foot of Castle Hill at Adam Clark Square (Clark Ádám tér) by the **Széchenyi Chain Bridge ❶** (Széchenyi Lánchíd). The Chain Bridge was Budapest's first stone bridge connecting the banks of the Danube, linking the towns of Buda and Pest together. Since then, the Chain Bridge has become synonymous with the city itself. The suspension bridge is considered by most to be the most beautiful in the capital, and is especially famed for its stone lions and its photogenic views up to the castle.

Looking across the Danube to Castle Hill

More than a century old, the bridge was constructed in the mid-1800s as a joint venture by Count István Széchenyi who proposed it, English engineer Tierney Clark and Scottish engineer Adam Clark (no rela-

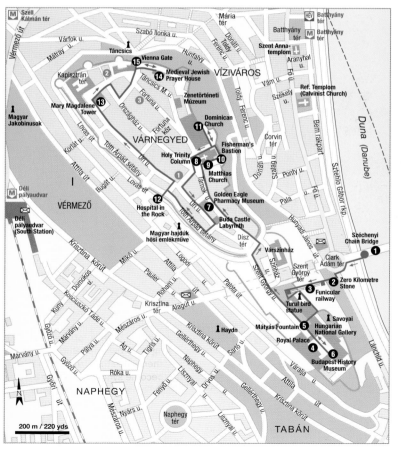

Budapest's funicular railway

tion). When the Germans blew up all of Budapest's bridges on 18 January 1945 at the end of World War II, the Chain Bridge was mostly destroyed, but underwent complete reconstruction four years later, exactly 100 years after its inauguration.

You can begin your walk by crossing the bridge on foot from Pest for a more dramatic opener, or start directly at bottom of Castle Hill in Adam Clark Square. Keep an eye out for the upright, elliptical piece of concrete, the **Zero Kilometre Stone ❷**, which marks the 0km point from which all Hungarian roads to and from the capital are measured, before taking the **funicular railway ❸** (*sikló*) up the hill.

This vintage contraption, decked out in mahogany and gold, was initially constructed in 1870 for the clerks who worked in the government offices up in the Castle District. Functioning on a pulley system, the two cars, Margit and Gellért – named for two of the city's famous saints – are used as counterweights; one car is hoisted up the cliff as the other descends. Like the Chain Bridge, the original funicular was damaged in the war. Today, its two stepped carriages are accurate copies of the originals.

When you exit the funicular up at Szent György tér, turn left for the Royal Palace. You can also reach Castle Hill on the number 16 bus (Várbusz), which will deposit you in Dísz tér – or take the healthy option and hike up the hill.

THE ROYAL PALACE (BUDA CASTLE)

What you see of the **Royal Palace ❹** (Budavári Palota) today is not actually very old. The castle has been destroyed 86 times over the course of history, and even today's Habsburg-looking structure is a post-war reconstruction. From the outside, the palace bears a close resemblance to its pre-war state; on the inside, however, the aesthetic is very much in line with a 1960s communist Social Realist style.

The entrance into the Royal Palace will bring you to the Habsburg steps. Towards the east you'll see the **Turul bird statue**, a bronze sculpture of a mythical bird resembling a hawk, constructed at the beginning of the 20th century. It's a totemic bird for the Hungarians, which, according to legend, impregnated the grandmother of Árpád, the chief military commander who led the Magyar tribes – the ancestors of today's Hungarians – into the Carpathian Basin in the late 800s. Heading past the ornamental gateway and descending the Habsburg steps will bring you out onto a grand terrace overlooking the river. Turn right, just below the copper-green dome that crowns the Royal Palace, and you'll find an entrance leading into the Hungarian National Gallery.

Hungarian National Gallery

Located inside the palace, the **Hungarian National Gallery** (Magyar

Hungarian National Gallery   *Budapest History Museum exhibit*

Nemzeti Galéria; www.mng.hu; Tue–Sun 10am–6pm) carries an extensive collection of Hungarian art. Dating from the 11th century to the modern day, the artworks spread out over four floors up to the dome itself.

The collection is curated chronologically, going up through the years as you climb the storeys of the Royal Palace. You'll find a comprehensive selection of winged altars, wooden sculptures and panel paintings from the 14th to 16th centuries, as well as medieval and Renaissance stone carvings, on the ground floor of the museum. Art from the 19th century, including several rooms dedicated to the work of Mihály Munkácsy, can be found on the first floor. Contemporary and modern art is exhibited on the second and third floors.

It's easy to spend hours in the Hungarian National Gallery alone, but alongside the permanent collection there are usually excellent temporary exhibitions held on the ground floor of the museum.

Mátyás Fountain

Exiting from the main entrance to the museum, cut across the palace by taking the path under the arches to your left. This will bring you to the neo-Baroque **Mátyás Fountain ❺**. Depicting King Mátyás Corvin, this fountain is sometimes dubbed as 'The Trevi Fountain of Budapest'. The bronze figures show the king and his hunting party in a theatrical composition; the water

cascades down the cracks in the boulders. The fountain dates back to the turn of the 20th century, and was only minimally damaged during World War II – one of the dogs was destroyed, but promptly restored.

Beyond the fountain, you'll find the **Budapest History Museum ❻** (Budapesti Történeti Múzeum; www.btm.hu; Tue–Fri 10am–4pm, Sat–Sun 10am–6pm), which is worth visiting if you're at all interested in learning about the city's history or want to take a peek at the Royal Palace's medieval past.

Afterwards, take the path back past the fountain towards the Corvinus Gate, an intricate iron gate topped with a raven – symbolising King Mátyás – and continue straight to Dísz tér.

TRINITY SQUARE

Take Dísz tér then Tárnok utca, the road forking to the right. En route, you'll pass the **Golden Eagle Pharmacy Museum ❼** (Arany Sas Patikamúzeum; http://semmelweismuseum.hu; seasonal hours – see website) located in a 15th-century house with a Baroque exterior, displaying medicinal tools and alchemy items from the Middle Ages.

Head straight on to Trinity Square (Szentháromság tér), which forms the heart of the historic district on Castle Hill. It is named for its Holy **Trinity Column ❽** (Szentháromság-Szobor), constructed in the early 18th century not only to commemorate the end of

Matthias Church

the plague, but to protect the people of Buda from future outbreaks. The original sculpture by Ceresola Vereio was removed in 1709 and relocated to another part of the city. In its place, a bigger and more elaborate monument by sculptor Fülöp Ungeleich was instated in 1713.

On the square, you'll also find the white Baroque **Old Town Hall of Buda** (Régi Budai Városháza), which became obsolete when the three cities of Buda, Óbuda and Pest merged into the capital – now known as Budapest – in 1873. To the north, the medieval-looking neo-Gothic building that houses the Hungarian Culture Foundation is actually 20th century.

Matthias Church

Lying at the heart of the square, the Church of Our Lady, better known as **Matthias Church ❾** (Mátyás Templom; Mon–Fri 9am–5pm, Sat until noon, Sun 1–5pm, although liturgies can affect regular hours), with its colourful rooftop mosaic of red, brown, green, white and mustard tiles, is the square's most notable building.

Like the district itself, the church is a tapestry of layers, constructed throughout the centuries. The original church was built in the 13th century under King Béla IV, although legend has it Saint István (Stephen) of Hungary founded the first church here in the 11th century, which was completely destroyed during the Mongol invasion. Much of what you see today originates from the 19th century, but at the bottom of Béla Tower you can still spot two medieval column heads. Note the pair of monks reading a book and the two demonic creatures fighting.

While the original church had the same dimensions as today's, it was significantly rebuilt in the 14th and 15th centuries, which saw the sidewalls lifted and the aisles lengthened; the 14th-century Mary Gate (Mária kapu) is the oldest part of the church. The church takes its name from King Mátyás, whose coronations and two weddings (first to Czech princess Katalin Podjebrád and then to Beatrix of Aragon) took place here in the 15th century. Many of the church's Renaissance elements, as well as the 60-metre (200ft) -high Mathias Bell Tower, bearing the Hunyadi family's coat of arms with the raven holding a gold ring in its beak, also date back to this period.

Under the Turkish occupation, the building functioned as a mosque. All the original frescoes and ornate furnishings were completely destroyed. In the 18th century, under Habsburg rule, the church incorporated Baroque elements, and then later in the 19th century, the neo-Gothic style by architect Frigyes Schulek that dominates the church today.

Fisherman's Bastion

Just off the square, **Fisherman's Bastion ❿** (Halászbástya) is one of Buda-

In the Fisherman's Bastion   *Ruszwurm Cukrászda coffee house*

pest's most photographed sites, and it's easy to see why. The fairy tale turrets adorned with colonnades and sculptures overlook the Danube River, with panoramas over the Hungarian Parliament building and the rest of Pest.

Despite its romantic neo-Romanesque airs, this lookout was never a part of Castle Hill's fortifications, but rather a late-19th-century medieval masquerade, constructed as a decorative viewing platform. This elegant structure bears seven turrets to symbolise the seven Hungarian tribes who settled in the Carpathian basin in 896. While the building itself is a copy by architect Frigyes Schulek, the man behind the later additions to Matthias Church, its name dates back to the Middle Ages, when the fishers' guild defended the castle wall in this very section.

The turrets, parapets, terraces and staircases offer the best views in the city, and while parts of the bastion are free to visit, the more spectacular sections require a small entrance fee.

Take a wander beyond Fisherman's Bastion into a hidden courtyard behind the Hilton Hotel to take in the Gothic remains of a 13th-century **Dominican church** ⓫.

BEYOND TRINITY SQUARE

Walk back to Trinity Square and turn down Szentháromság utca. If you're in the mood for refreshments, the **Ruszwurm Cukrászda**, see ❶, is a good place to grab a cake and a coffee before turning left down the cobbled Úri utca, lined with colourful Baroque houses. Turn right into Móra Ferenc utca and head right for a stroll down Tóth Árpád sétány, a leafy promenade with views over towards the Buda Hills in the distance. Continue on until you come to a stairway, leading you down on the left-hand side, which will bring you out onto Lovas út. Head right until you reach the entrance to the Hospital in the Rock.

Hospital in the Rock

Beneath Buda Castle there is a complex network of tunnels, caves and cellars that measure around 10km (6 miles). Part of these caves are natural, the main part being found in the **Buda Castle Labyrinth** (Budavári Labirintus; www.labirintus.eu; daily 10am–7pm) complex. A major section of this cave system was reinforced for use as a bomb shelter.

Since Castle Hill was a government district, the mayor of the city, Dr Károly Szendy, ordered that the **Hospital in the Rock** ⓬ (Sziklakórház; www.sziklakorhaz.eu; daily 10am–7pm) be created. The hospital, opened in 1944, lies in mostly man-made tunnels that connected to the natural caves, and was originally constructed to offer emergency care for residents, civilians and soldiers in the district. During World War II, and particularly during the Siege of Buda, the hospi-

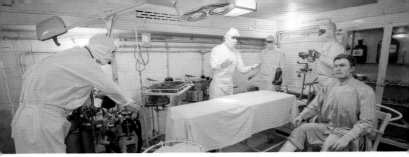

Eerie waxworks at the Hospital in the Rock

tal, built to serve 300 people, became overcrowded with some 700 patients, many of whom had to lie in the sub-terranean corridors of the hospital. Today, you can visit the hospital on a one-hour guided tour, which will take you through the various surgeries and rooms, brought to life by creepy, life-like waxwork figures – the only part of the exhibit that is not original.

After World War II and the 1956 uprising, the hospital fell into disuse and morphed into a nuclear bunker during the Cold War period. The interior was converted to withstand a chemical or nuclear attack, thanks to its inter-nal ventilation and poison gas-filtering system, coupled with a power gener-ator. For decades, the former hospital became part of the civil-defence infra-structure until its declassification in 2002. It opened as a museum in 2007, after being modernised and restored. It is one of Budapest's most unusual museums, offering a curious insight into the city's 20th-century history.

Magdalene Tower

Return back up the stairs and continue down Szentháromság utca and turn left. Keep walking down Úri utca until you reach Kapisztrán tér, with the **Mary Magdalene Tower** ⑱ (Mária Magdolna Torony) and its surrounding ruins. The original Mary Magdalene Church was built in the 13th century for Hungari-an-speaking worshipers, and was one of the only churches not converted

into a mosque during the Ottoman occupation. Most of the structure was destroyed by bombing during World War II, which left only the 15th-century tower standing. You'll find plenty of places to grab a bite to eat or drink in the vicinity, such as at **Baltazár Budapest**, see ❷, or **Pierrot Cafe & Restaurant**, see ❸.

Medieval synagogue

Continuing down towards Bécsi Kapu tér, it's easy to feel that the Castle Dis-trict is dominated by Baroque residen-tial houses away from the Royal Palace, but take a turn down Táncsics Mihály utca to number 26 to catch a glimpse of the old **Medieval Jewish Prayer House** ⑭, known as the Bethel. Exca-vated in the 1960s, from the outside the building blends in with the rest of the street. It was constructed at the end of the 14th century, and you can still see some original features from the old medieval prayer house. The synagogue was mostly used in the 16th and 17th centuries by the Sephardic Jews who came to Buda in the wake of the Otto-man conquest. Opposite at number 23, a larger and older synagogue lies under-ground, awaiting excavation.

While many associate Budapest's Jewish Quarter with the one in central Pest, during the 13th century many Jews came to Hungary during the reign of King Béla IV, who offered them the freedom to worship and the right to a house of prayer. The streets around Szent György utca, close to today's

Royal Palace, once made up the old Jewish quarter, but the community were forced to leave under the reign of King Lajos IV, only to return to Buda in the mid-14th century. The synagogue was converted into an apartment after the Habsburg-led army massacred many of the Jews following the Ottoman occupation, and it was forgotten about until its excavation.

Vienna Gate

Return to the **Vienna Gate** ⓑ (Bécsi kapu) to finish the route. This reconstructed gate has a symbolic significance rather than a functional one, with its inscriptions, reliefs and ornamentation. In the Middle Ages, the original gate earned the name 'Saturday Gate' (Szombat kapu) due to the weekly markets that took place here. In the 19th century, the original gate was demolished. Today's dates from 1936 and memorialises the 250th anniversary of Buda's recapture from the Turks.

The square marks the end of the Castle District, with roads and buses leading down to Széll Kálmán tér, which has connections to take you back into the city centre.

Food and Drink

❶ RUSZWURM CUKRÁSZDA

Szentháromság utca 7; tel: 1 375 5284; www.ruszwurm.hu; daily 10am–7pm; €
This little coffee house is the oldest in Budapest. Founded in 1827, it serves classic Hungarian cakes, such as decadent *krémes*, a cream cake wedged in between flaky pastry topped with dusting sugar or caramel, or *dobos torte*, a traditional Hungarian chocolate cake crowned with a hardened caramel layer. If you're in the mood for something savoury, try the *pogácsa* – scones made with cheese or pork fat.

❷ BALTAZÁR BUDAPEST

Országház utca 31; tel: 1 300 7050; http://baltazarbudapest.com; daily 7.30am–11pm; €€

First and foremost a boutique and design hotel, Baltazár Budapest also houses the excellent Hungarian Grill Restaurant and Wine bar, where charcoal-grilled meats and gourmet street food are the stars. In addition to this, the restaurant offers an extensive selection of Hungarian and Central European wines, as well as quality spirits and cocktails.

❸ PIERROT CAFE & RESTAURANT

Fortuna utca 14; tel: 1 375 6971; http://pierrot.hu; daily noon–midnight; €€€
This fine-dining establishment, set in a 13th-century old bakery house, has seen its share of celebrity guests. A culinary institution on Castle Hill for three decades, this is the place to enjoy Hungarian cuisine with a refined twist. Specials include its own unique take on the classic goulash, made using venison.

St Stephen's Basilica

PARLIAMENT AND AROUND

Pest's Inner City (Belváros) made up the foundations of the medieval city of Pest. Today, the area is dominated by elegant buildings, fine dining and high-end shops, lying at the heart of the city's government quarter.

DISTANCE: 5km (3 miles)
TIME: A full day
START: St Stephen's Basilica
END: Károly Garden
POINTS TO NOTE: If you don't want to walk the entire way, you can hop on the number 2 tram, which follows most of the route along the Danube from the Hungarian Parliament building.

While Buda occupies hilly terrain on the other side of the Danube, Pest is completely flat. And while Buda was part of the Roman Empire, the Danube marked the border, leaving Pest outside of Roman jurisdiction, except for the fortress Contra Aquincum, whose ruins you can still spot in Március 15 tér.

In the 15th century, Pest became a free town and caught up with Buda to become the second-largest settlement in the country; it grew into a thriving trade centre enclosed by a city wall. You can still see part of the old wall if you wander through Budapest's inner streets. Much of the city's development halted during the Ottoman occupation, and was only revived in the 18th century when many of the original buildings and city walls were demolished or incorporated into newer buildings. Today, it's an elegant district peppered with classical buildings, squares and a breezy promenade running along the Danube.

This central area lies within the V District, but it's made up of two neighbourhoods: Belváros and Lipótváros. The former is characterised by this older part of the city once enclosed within the city walls, whereas the latter is home to some of Budapest's most iconic sites, like the Hungarian Parliament and St Stephen's Basilica.

ST STEPHEN'S BASILICA

Begin your walk at **St Stephen's Basilica ❶** (Szent István Bazilika; http://en.bazilika.biz; Mon–Sat 9am–7pm, Sun 7.45am–7pm). Budapest's neoclassical cathedral is one of most photographed spots in the city. Along with the Hungarian Parliament building, St Stephen's Basilica is the joint-tall-

Basilica door detail

The ornate interior of St Stephen's Basilica

est building in the city at 96 metres (315ft). Hungarian regulations maintain that no building can exceed this height; the buildings – representing church and state – dominate the skyline with equal standing.

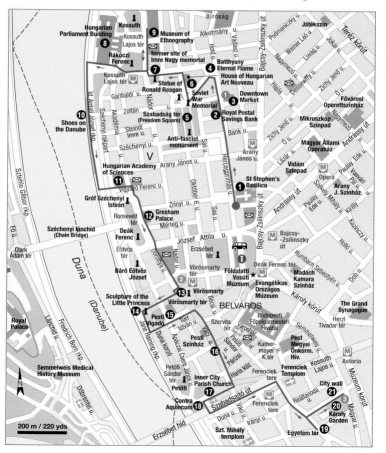

Soviet War Memorial

Initially designed by József Hild, planned by architect Miklós Ybl and completed by József Kauser, the Basilica was finally finished in 1905 after taking more than half a century to build – in 1868 a storm destroyed the dome, and the entire construction had to be built again from the ground up. Today, it's an impressive building structured in a Greek cross plan, anchored with two large bell towers flanking the dome.

You can enter the Basilica and ascend the viewing platform for 360° views across the city. The treasury on the second floor has an impressive collection of ecclesiastical objects, but the most famous relic is the mummified right hand of St Stephen, Hungary's canonised king, which is located in the Sacred Right Chapel (Szent Jobb Kápolna).

Turn right upon exiting the Basilica and continue straight down Herceg-prímás utca and Hold utca.

Royal Postal Savings Bank

It's impossible to miss this Secessionist wonder on Hold utca. Just look up and marvel at the green and yellow tiled roof that crowns Ödön Lechner's architectural masterpiece. Originally the **Royal Postal Savings Bank**  (Postatakarék-pénztár), today it houses the Hungarian State Treasury, was built in 1901 as Hungary's answer to Gaudí. There is so much detail to take in, from the winged serpents intertwined with the side tower to the Hungarian floral folk motifs.

Downtown Market

Opposite the Royal Postal Savings Bank, the **Downtown Market** ❸ (Belvárosi Piac) is a modern market hall that brings the best of Hungarian gastronomy from the countryside into the heart of the city. You'll find the usual suspects intermixed with Hungarian specialities like Mangalica pork and grey-cattle beef. Stop here to grab a bite, from street food to rustic bites with a gourmet twist, such as at the **A Séf Utcája**, see ❶.

FREEDOM SQUARE

Continue down the street to reach Aulich utca. Pause here to check out the **Batthyany Eternal Flame** (Batthyany Orokmecses) ❹, a stone lantern containing a small, bronze oil lantern that pays tribute to Count Lajos Battyány, the prime minister of Hungary's first independent government following the

Statue of Ronald Reagan

House of Art Nouveau   *Inside the House of Hungarian Art Nouveau*

Revolution of 1848. Battyány was executed in 1849 in neighbouring Freedom Square after being arrested by the Habsburgs and tried as a traitor.

Turn down the street and you'll come out onto **Freedom Square** ❺ (Szabadság tér), one of the largest open spaces in central Budapest. The square is dominated by a large park that sets the stage for summer festivals, protests and events, flanked by neoclassical buildings, such as the Exchange Palace, once the headquarters for Hungarian Television (MTV), which vacated the premises in 2009. Today, the building is privately owned and will be redeveloped into prime retail and office space.

Controversial memorials

You'll also find various memorials in the square. On one side, you'll see the surreal **statue of Ronald Reagan** by Vécsey utca, and on the other there is the **Anti-fascist monument**, built in 2014, which has been a controversial talking point ever since. The monument, depicting the Archangel Gabriel being attacked by a German Imperial Eagle, is dedicated to 'all the victims' of Hungary's German occupation. However, the monument garnered criticism from those who claimed it whitewashed Hungary's role in the Holocaust. Directly in front of the official monument, a poignant, alternative memorial composed of candles, letters and personal relics, laid by protesters and relatives of Holocaust victims, lies in quiet protest.

On the northern side of Freedom Square, you'll see the imposing **Soviet War Memorial**, dedicated to the Soviet army. This obelisk-like structure was erected in 1946 by the Soviet Army to mark the last resting place of the Russians who fell during Budapest's liberation from the Germans. The monument is crowned with a gold star and surrounded by reliefs of the Soviet troops in action. Despite the two nations' troubled history, Hungary has signed an agreement to protect this contentious memorial.

House of Hungarian Art Nouveau

If you continue away from the Soviet War Memorial down Honvéd utca, you'll come to the museum – **House of Hungarian Art Nouveau** ❻ (Magyar Szecesszió Háza; www.magyarszecessziohaza.hu; Mon–Sat 10am–5pm), featuring ceramics and furniture from the era, as well as a café. This applegreen building, built by Emil Vidor in 1903, comes with all the organic intricacies associated with the style. The apartment block was built for industrialist and art-collector Béla Bedő (the house also goes by the name Bedő House).

KOSSÚTH LAJOS SQUARE

Continue down Honvéd utca and turn left at Báthory utca, heading towards Kossúth tér. En route, you'll pass the former site of the **memorial dedicated to Imre Nagy** ❼. The memorial was removed in 2018 and relocated to

The striking Hungarian Parliament Building

Jászai Mari Square. The bronze statue stood on the bridge, looking towards the Hungarian Parliament. Former Prime Minister Imre Nagy was a key figure in the 1956 uprising, who dreamt of a Hungary free from Stalin and the Soviet Union. He was removed from Parliament in 1955 for his 'controversial' views.

The bullet holes from the 25 October uprising can still be seen in the nearby Ministry of Agriculture, when secret police opened fire on thousands protesting outside the Parliament. Nagy was eventually arrested and executed after being condemned to death in a secret trial. The controversial removal of the statue was part of a plan to return the square to its pre-war look. However, some have argued that the removal was rather meant to re-write history.

Turn right on the corner to come to Kossúth Lajos Square (Kossuth Lajos tér) and the spectacular Hungarian Houses of Parliament.

Hungarian Parliament

The imposing **Hungarian Parliament Building** ❽ (Országház; http://hungarianparliament.com; May–Sept Mon–Fri 8am–6pm, Sat until 4pm, Sun until 2pm, Oct–Apr Mon–Sat 8am–4pm, Sun until 2pm) is the seat of Hungary's National Government and one of the oldest legislative buildings in Europe.

Built by Imre Steindl, who won an international competition to design the building in the late 19th century, the Parliament is constructed in dramatic neo-Gothic revival style, with prickly spires, symmetrical wings and a central dome, mirroring the Royal Palace on the other side of the Danube. If the Hungarian Parliament Building recalls London's Houses of Parliament, it's no coincidence, since the architect drew inspiration from its British counterpart.

The structure is made of 40 million bricks, 40kg (88lb) of gold and almost half a million precious stones. Its numerous statues depict Hungarian rulers and famous figures. In order to mark the 1000th anniversary of Hungary as a state, the building was inaugurated in 1896. Like St Stephen's Basilica, the dome reaches a height of 96 metres (315ft).

You can visit the Parliament building on a guided tour, which includes traipsing the grand staircase and perusing stained glass and mosaics by Miksa Róth. Book a tour in advance if possible.

Museum of Ethnography

Opposite the Hungarian Houses of Parliament is another grand building, the **Museum of Ethnography** ❾ (Néprajzi Múzeum; www.neprajz.hu/en; Tue–Sun 10am–6pm). This building, by architect Alajos Hauszmann, was constructed in 1897 in neo-Renaissance style, with classical columns and statues of legislators and magistrates – honouring the building's past as a Palace of Justice.

Enjoying a guided tour of Parliament

Inside, the building is just as spectacular, and houses a collection of folk art and costumes from rural Hungary and the surrounding regions. The building served as a backdrop in the film *Evita*, starring Madonna, shot in Budapest in the mid-1990s.

ALONG THE DANUBE

Come out of the Museum of Ethnography and turn right then left, following the square round to take the stairs down from Kossuth Lajos tér on the left-hand side of the Parliament Building. Take the zebra crossing over the Id. Antall József rakpart to the river bank.

Shoes on the Danube
Turn left and keep walking until you reach the **Shoes on the Danube** ❿ memorial. In 1944, Hitler overthrew Hungary's leader and replaced him with Ferenc Szalasi, who established the Arrow Cross Party, a fascist and anti-Semitic organisation. Budapest's Jewish population was rounded up, with 80,000 deported to concentration camps and 20,000 shot into the Danube. At gunpoint, the Jews were forced to remove their shoes, which were a valuable commodity, before being shot by a firing squad into the freezing water.

Today, the memorial – of iron shoes lined up along the Danube – is simple, yet so poignant. The 60 pairs are realistic, detailed and made of metal in period style, created by film director Can Togay and sculptor Gyula Pauer.

Hungarian Academy of Sciences
Continue along the promenade away from the Parliament building until you reach the zebra crossing close to Chain Bridge. Along the way, you'll get wonderful views across to Buda; there are plenty of benches under the trees further up if you feel like taking a rest.

Once you've crossed, take time to admire the **Hungarian Academy of Sciences** ⓫ (Magyar Tudományos Akadémia), established by Count István Széchenyi in 1825. It's still the seat for the prestigious Learned Society of Hungary. The Academy was built in 1865 by Friedrich August Stüler.

Gresham Palace
Across the leafy green park at the heart of Széchenyi István tér sits the Art Nouveau wonder that is **Gresham Palace** ⓬, home to the prestigious Four Seasons Hotel. This spectacular building, by Zsigmond Quittner and József Vágo, was once a luxury block of apartments with prime viewing over to the Chain bridge. It earned its name from the London Gresham Insurance Company who erected the building.

On the inside, a gate laced with wrought-iron peacocks expands into an arcade topped with glass, as well as mosaics and ceramic tiles from the Zsolnay factory. The entrance can be visited even if you're not a guest, and there's also a café open to the public.

Outside seating at Vörösmarty tér

Vörösmarty tér

Head down Dorottya utca to **Vörösmarty tér** ⓭, an elegant square that comes to life with events and festivals, such as the Christmas Market. While the square is mostly famous for shopping, it's also a gastro hub, home to Michelin-starred **Onyx**, see ❷.

Continue down towards the Duna Corsó, filled with more cafés and restaurants. You'll see the bronze **sculpture of the Little Princess** ⓮

(kiskirálylány szobor) perched on the railings by the Danube.

Pesti Vigadó

Opposite the Little Princess is the grand **Pesti Vigadó** ⓯ (www.pestivigado.hu; daily 10am–7pm). Built in 1864, this Romantic-style concert hall is still in use today, having been reconstructed following World War II damage. It's a cultural hub that offers classical concerts in its main hall, with a spectacular terrace that opens up above the Danube. There are also interesting exhibitions. Try to visit on a guided tour.

INSIDE THE INNER CITY WALLS

Head up towards **Váci utca** ⓰, one of Budapest's main shopping thoroughfares – you've now entered the historic old city. You'll find a mix of tourist shops and high-end design and fashion stores along this street. Continue on until you reach the arch-covered walkway and turn down Piarista köz. This will bring you out onto Március 15 tér.

Március 15 tér

At the head of the square is the **Inner City Parish Church** ⓱ (Belvárosi plébánia templom). This is the oldest church in Pest, founded in the 11th century, and the alleged resting place of St Gellért. The building was refurbished in Gothic style in the 14th century, and then in Renaissance in the 16th, as well as altering significantly under Ottoman occu-

The opulent Pesti Vigadó

pation. Like many others, this church became a mosque, and you can still see the original Turkish mihrab inside. Later on, the church was refurbished in the Baroque style you see today.

Outside the church, before you take the crossing under Elizabeth Bridge, keep an eye out for the ruins of **Contra Aquincum** (18).

Egyetem tér and Károly Garden

Head straight up Kossuth Lajos utca and turn right, heading towards Egyetem tér. This part of the Inner City has recently been renovated and cleaned up, showcasing beautiful neoclassical and neo-Renaissance styles. At its heart, you'll find **Egyetem tér** (19) (University Square), an open square that leads out to the charming **Károly Garden** (20) (Károly Kert).

The garden is enclosed with vintage iron railings, and can be accessed during daylight hours. It's a quiet, elegant sanctuary, away from the hustle and bustle of city life. On the corner, you'll find the terrace belonging to **Csendes Társ**, see (3), in the summer. This is also one of the few places where you can spot the original **city wall** (21), which has been built into the façades of the buildings in the vicinity. Here you can end your walk with a rest in the park, or head back into the Jewish Quarter or Palace District.

Food and Drink

(1) A SÉF UTCÁJA

Hold utca 13; tel: 70 390 7757; www.facebook.com/asefutcaja; Mon 11.30am–4.30pm, Tue–Fri until 5.30pm, Sat until 4pm; €
A Séf Utcája, which translates as 'The Chef's Street', is located inside the Downtown Market. This deli and bistro serves traditional meat cuts and local dishes with a trendy twist.

(2) ONYX

Vörösmarty tér 7; tel: 30 508 0622; www.onyxrestaurant.hu; Tue–Wed 6.30–11pm; Thu–Sat noon–2.30pm and 6.30–11pm; €€€

This two Michelin-starred restaurant is one of Budapest's best fine-dining establishments. The menu offers a modern reimagining of Hungarian dishes, along with an impressive collection of local and international wines. You can also take advantage of their special four or six-course lunch menu.

(3) CSENDES TÁRS

Magyar utca 18; tel: 30 727 2100; www.csend.es/CsendesTars; daily 10am–10pm; €
Csendes Társ is a café, wine bar and restaurant in the square right next to the wrought-iron gates of Károly Garden. During the summer, Csendes takes things outdoors, but up the road, Csendes Vintage Bar & Café is open all year.

The Great Synagogue

THE JEWISH QUARTER

The Jewish Quarter (Zsidó Negyed) mixes up past and present. Its dilapidated buildings embrace their shabby-chic aesthetic with trendy ruin bars, design shops and hip cafés that thread alongside the district's synagogues and Holocaust memorials.

DISTANCE: 3km (1.8 miles)
TIME: A full day
START: Great Synagogue
END: Szimpla Kert
POINTS TO NOTE: The synagogues are closed for the Sabbath on Saturdays. If you choose to do the route on a Sunday, you may want to start at Szimpla Kert instead, as there is a great farmers' market on until 2pm.

Buda had a thriving Jewish community under the rule of King Béla IV (1235–70). However, following the Siege of Buda in 1686 – when the Habsburgs overthrew the Turks – the Jewish population was expelled until Maria Theresa's son, Joseph II, ended the prohibition in 1783. At this time, 14 families lived in the Orczy mansion, located just outside Pest's city walls. Their numbers increased rapidly, with Jews coming from Óbuda and other parts of the Habsburg Empire. In the 19th and early 20th centuries, the district flourished with synagogues and houses, and the population continued to grow.

During World War II, in the summer of 1944, the Arrow Cross Party rounded up Jews across the city and put them in designated Yellow Star Houses, where they awaited deportation to the concentration camps. More than 2,000 Yellow Star Houses appeared in Budapest, most of which were located within the quarter. In the winter, a Jewish ghetto was established, cramming 70,000 people into an area of less than a square mile.

Following the war and the Holocaust, the district was left mostly abandoned, with houses in poor condition. Much of it was ripe for redevelopment until Szimpla Kert set up shop in one of the deserted buildings, becoming among the most popular bars in the city. Soon, other ruin bars opened up and the area was transformed into a trendy hub for young creatives. It has since become one of the most fashionable areas and hottest nightlife spots in the city. Today, you'll find ruin bars side by side with crumbling buildings and chic design shops. But even as you walk around this trendy district it's impossible to miss the area's fascinating – and often haunting – past.

Raoul Wallenberg Memorial

The Great Synagogue's main hall

AROUND THE GREAT SYNAGOGUE

Begin your walk outside the Great Synagogue, close to Astoria at the beginning of Dohány utca. Before going inside, make sure you admire this grand Moorish Revival building, from its two towers measuring over 40-metres (130ft) high, topped with onion-shaped domes accented with a hint of gold, to the Hebrew inscription above the door. Built in the mid-1800s, this synagogue is truly unique – German architect Ludwig Förster believed that Jewish architecture could not be distinctly identified, so instead created a fusion of styles from the Middle East to North Africa

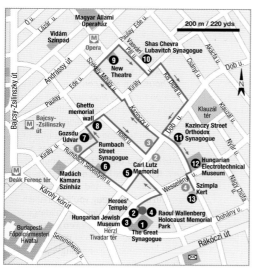

to the Alhambra. However, following its positive reception, Moorish Revival architecture went on to influence other synagogues in the city.

Great Synagogue

Queue up at the entrance for tickets to go inside the complex. **The Great Synagogue** ❶ (Dohány utcai Zsinagóga; www.dohany-zsinagoga.hu; last week of Apr–Sept Sun–Thu 10am–8pm, Fri until 4pm, Nov–Feb Sun–Thu 10am–4pm, Fri until 2pm, Mar–end of Apr and Oct Sun–Thu 10am-6pm, Fri until 4pm, closed on Jewish holidays), also known as the Dohány Street Synagogue, is the largest synagogue in Europe, and the second largest in the world. It has the capacity to seat 3,000 people in a grand hall that measures 1,200 sq metres (12,900 sq ft). Consecrated in 1859, with the exterior by Förster and the interior by Hungarian architect Frigyes Feszl, the grandeur and size of the synagogue demonstrates the significance of Budapest's Jewish community at the time.

The interior is split into a gallery for women upstairs, and men downstairs, and is no less impressive than the exterior, with its spectacular pipe organ, central

Some of the displays at the Hungarian Jewish Museum were donated by city residents

rose window, hanging chandeliers and accents of gold set against a bright palette of reds, blues, greens and yellows.

The Great Synagogue is the temple of Neolog Jewry, a mild reform movement within Judaism originating in the late 19th century and occurring mainly in Hungarian-speaking regions. Since Orthodox Judaism during that period was stricter concerning the use of modern innovations, Neolog Judaism sought to embrace a more contemporary lifestyle, with the intention of blending in with the local community. Most Hungarian Neolog Jews adopted Hungarian in place of Yiddish as their primary language, viewing themselves as Hungarians who happened to follow a Jewish religion.

The location of the synagogue marked the beginning of the Jewish ghetto in World War II, and its garden became a makeshift cemetery for 2,600 Jews who perished here during the Holocaust. The building was also damaged by 27 bombings during the war, and was restored with funding from actor Tony Curtis and his daughter Jamie Lee Curtis, who are of Hungarian-Jewish descent.

Men can obtain a *yamaka* from the person at the synagogue's entrance, and there is also a security bag check.

Heroes' Temple

Just behind the synagogue but within the complex, the **Heroes' Temple ❷**, by László Vágo, was built much later than the main synagogue and in a slightly different style. Erected in 1931, it recalls Ancient Babylonia on the outside. This small prayer house also commemorates the 10,000 Jewish soldiers who fought in World War I.

After the collapse of the Austro-Hungarian empire following World War I, Hungary fell to pieces. Certain politically influential figures and circles blamed the country's minorities. In response, the Jewish community wanted to prove its loyalty, so collected information about those soldiers who fought bravely for their country, giving the community an incentive to build the Heroes' Temple as a memorial. The temple also functions as a winter synagogue, when the main building is not heated.

While you can't go inside the Heroes' Temple, you can catch a glimpse of the interior through its doors.

Jewish Museum

The **Hungarian Jewish Museum ❸** (Magyar Zsidó Múzeum; http://enmi lev.weebly.com; May–Sept Sun–Thu 10am–6pm, Fri until 4pm, Nov–Feb Sun–Thu 10am–4pm, Fri until 2pm, Oct, Mar, Apr Sun–Thu 10am–8pm, Fri until 4pm, closed on Jewish holidays) presents the history of the local Jewish community. It was created 80 years after the foundation of the synagogue, but still follows its exterior aesthetic; the interior, by contrast, is bright and modern. The original museum opened in a private apartment in 1916, based on an initiative of Jewish intellectuals

who collected various objects relevant to Hungarian Jewish history. Families and individuals also donated anything they felt was worthy of belonging to the collection. As such, there's an eclectic and curious range of pieces.

Pick up an audio guide at the entrance, free of charge.

Raoul Wallenberg Memorial Garden

Upon exiting the complex, you'll pass the **Raoul Wallenberg Holocaust Memorial Park ❹**, with its memorial tree envisioned by Tony Curtis and designed by sculptor Imre Varga. The metal sculpture is a poignant memorial; each leaf of this weeping willow bears the name of victims who died in the Holocaust.

The tree is named after Raoul Wallenberg, a Swedish diplomat credited with saving thousands of Jews threatened with deportation. Using Sweden's political neutrality, Wallenberg offered diplomatic immunity to Jewish families by issuing them 'Wallenberg Passports' which extended protection – those with Wallenberg Passports did not have to wear a yellow star. When the Arrow Cross forced Jews into the ghetto, Wallenberg hung the Swedish flag from approximately 30 houses in the Újlipótváros neighbourhood, rendering them safe houses for some 15,000 Jews. The exact number is not known, but it is believed that Wallenberg helped up to 100,000 Jews.

Besides the tree, there's a turnstile leading out of the complex into Wesselényi utca. Turn right and keep walking straight until you reach Síp utca, turn left, and when you reach Dob utca, turn left again. You'll pass the entrance to Gozsdu Udvar, which you'll walk through later. Keep going until you reach another memorial, tucked into the corner of Ernö Lestyán's red-brick transformer station.

The **Carl Lutz memorial ❺** shows a figure lying on the floor, reaching up to a bronze suspended from a perpendicular wall, connected by a metallic roll of cloth. This piece commemorates a Swiss Vice Consul who, like Raoul Wallenberg, saved thousands of Jews during the Holocaust (more than 60,000 to be precise). The memorial dates to the early 1990s, and marks the former entrance to the Budapest ghetto.

RUMBACH SEBESTYÉN UTCA

At the corner of the transformer station and Rumbach Sebestyén utca, turn right and continue straight. Make sure you stop and take a glance at the art on the firewalls as you do, with one work depicting the famous Hungarian Rubik's Cube and the other of Ferenc Puskás, Hungary's most famous football player.

Rumbach Sebestyén Synagogue

Similar to the Great Synagogue, the **Rumbach Street Synagogue ❻** (closed due to renovation until early 2020) bears the same Moorish Revival architecture, with minaret-like towers and Orientalist designs. In the 19th

The Moorish Revival Rumbach Sebestyén Synagogue

century, Hungary's Jewish community became divided into Orthodox and Neolog Jews, but some refused to join either group, forming the 'Status Quo Ante' community of modern conservative Jews. This synagogue was built in 1872 by Austrian Secessionist architect Otto Wagner.

The interior is an explosion of colour, with blue, red and gold embossments on the wall, and intricate rose windows set about the octagonal dome and Moorish-style friezes. Much of the building was damaged during the war, and in 1959, when the community dwindled, the synagogue was closed and deconsecrated. It was sold off to a private buyer and has only recently been reacquired by the Jewish community. Since then it has functioned solely as a museum and not as a place of worship.

GOZSDU UDVAR AND KIRÁLY UTCA

Along this street you'll also find some fun and quirky shops, like Printa, a silkscreen print and upcycled fashion design shop. But continue straight on until you reach the intersection at Madách Imre utca. There are plenty of cafés and restaurants around here – **Konyha**, see ❶, is a particularly popular spot for lunch.

Gozsdu Udvar
Turn right up Madách Imre utca and continue until you reach the heart of Gozsdu Udvar ❼. Named after Romanian lawyer Manó Gozsdu, this complex of interconnected courtyards was built in the early 20th century by Győző Czigler. The name Gozsdu Udvar translates as 'Gozsdu Courtyards'. The complex once played a key role in local Jewish life, almost functioning as a self-contained community. You'd not only find shops and stores here, but even the first prayer houses in the area. Today, it's become a trendy hub of restaurants and cafés. If you're lucky, you may also find a vintage and antiques market held here (on weekends or national holidays) selling everything from communist memorabilia to crafted soaps and local contemporary design.

Turn left as you enter from Madách Imre utca and you'll find yourself on Király utca. This street marks the boundary that divides the VI and VII districts; it also once marked the edge of the ghetto. During the time of the Arrow Cross Party, it was very dangerous for Jews to be caught wandering around Király utca. Today, the street is unrecognisable. Instead, you'll find throngs of partygoers at night. During the day, it's a popular thoroughfare famed for its design shops, interior design stores and fashion boutiques.

The Ghetto memorial wall
When you enter Király utca, turn right and stop at number 15. Peek through the gate to the **Ghetto memorial wall** ❽ at the back of the courtyard. This is not the genuine ghetto wall, but rather a memo-

Market in Gozsdu Udvar

rial that's been built on the spot where the original stood. Most of the ghetto was closed off by the actual houses of the district or with wooden fencing. However, parts of the ghetto were enclosed by a stone wall, such as this one, which was rebuilt in 2010 using the stones from the original.

Continue down Király utca, turning right at Holló utca and then left at Dob utca. You'll find a few places to grab a bite to eat here, like shabby-chic and romantic **Vintage Garden**, see ➋. Alternatively, try a traditional Hungarian-Jewish pastry at **Fröhlich Kóser Cukrászda**, see ➌.

Turn left down Kazinczy, another street popular for its bars and *kerts* (open-air bars). Make sure you take time to appreciate the street art along here.

CROSSING INTO THE VI DISTRICT

Continue straight on, cross Király utca and head into the VI District. Take a right at Paulay Ede utca, and stop in front of the New Theatre.

New Theatre
Look up at the ornate façade of the **New Theatre ➒**, with hints of blue and gold and its name spelled out in lapis lazuli, with feminine faces set against geometric lines. This Art Nouveau building was constructed in 1908 by Béla Lajta. Initially, there was a night club here, the Parisiana Music Hall, but today it houses a respected theatre.

Continue down the street before turning right into Vasvári Pál utca, making sure you stop in front of the synagogue hidden in a courtyard.

Shas Chevra Lubavitch Synagogue
The Vásvári Pál Street Synagogue, also known as the **Shas Chevra Lubavitch Synagogue ➓** (Szász Chevra Lubavicsi zsinagóga), was completed in 1887 for the Talmud Society of Budapest. It's surrounded by a U-shape of residential buildings that were initially constructed and inhabited by members of the society. The complex also once housed a library and an academic institution. The more conservative Jews, who did not support the reform ideas of the Pest Jews, founded a new organisation in 1842 called the Talmud Association (Sasz Chevra). The intent of this group was to keep the traditions of, and teach from, the Talmud.

Since the 1990s, the Chabad Lubavits community started to use this synagogue. It is not normally open to the public, but it's worth peering through the gate when walking down here.

After the synagogue, continue down to turn left on Király utca and then right into Kis Diófa utca.

THE HEART OF THE JEWISH QUARTER

You'll soon arrive at Klauzál Square (Klauzál tér), a green leafy park with an impressive market hall on its other side.

Kazinczy Street Orthodox Synagogue

This square marks the heart of the Jewish Quarter. Until the late 19th century, there was a theatre on the site where the renovated market now stands.

Turn down Dob utca and continue until you reach Kazinczy utca again. Instead of going down to the right (you've already been there), turn left to head towards another impressive synagogue.

Kazinczy Street Orthodox Synagogue

If the Jewish shops selling memorabilia and menorahs weren't a clue enough, take a look up from the cobbled street to the elaborate red-bricked building where the road curves round. You may notice the Hebrew lettering – in Art Nouveau style – at the top denoting the **Kazinczy Street Orthodox Synagogue** ⓫ (Kazinczy utcai zsinagóga; Mon–Thu 10am–3.30pm, Fri and Sun 10am–12.30pm, closed on Jewish holidays). This is one of the later synagogues in the district, having been completed in 1912–3 by Sándor and Béla Löffler. It represents the third branch of 19th-century Judaism in Budapest – the Orthodox – the strictest and most tradition-bound community.

The interior of the synagogue impresses with its sky-blue ceiling, carved benches and decorative elements that draw inspiration from Hungarian folk art. The complex itself includes a house of worship, headquarters, a kosher butcher, a nursery, a Talmud school and a *mikveh* (Jewish ritual bath).

Synagogue etiquette

When visiting Budapest's synagogues, it's important to be respectful. Men cannot enter without wearing a cap or a hat, ideally a *yamaka* or *kippah*. You will usually be given a temporary cap after ticket inspection. Remember to dress appropriately too – so no sleeveless tops, shorts or short skirts. Turn your mobile phone on silent (or off) and avoid speaking loudly. The rules are more relaxed when visiting on a tour, as you will not be attending during congregations. If you're in doubt about specific etiquette, your guide can advise you.

Hungarian Electrotechnical Museum

Continue down the cobbled street until you come to one of Budapest's most unusual museums, the **Hungarian Electrotechnical Museum** ⓬ (Magyar Elektrotechnikai Múzeum; Tue–Sat 11am–7pm), which offers curious exhibits on Hungarian electrical engineering. You can learn how the alarm system used on the Austria-Hungary border worked, as well as taking a look at vintage appliances and old-school neon signs.

Szimpla Kert

Further down the road, end your tour at the famous **Szimpla Kert** ⓭ (http://szimpla.hu; Mon–Sat noon–4am, Sun

9am–4am). If you're feeling hungry, pop into **Karavan**, see ❹, for some street food next door.

Szimpla was Budapest's original ruin bar; its opening in the early 2000s was the turning point for the district. It's a quirky place that feels dilapidated, yet it's also invigorated with contemporary art work, vintage furniture and creative lighting. But what will strike you most is the sheer scale of the place – it was once an apartment complex, whose flats and rooms have been opened up. Szimpla makes for a mellow spot to enjoy a drink in the afternoon, or – if you're looking for the party – come on a Friday or Saturday night when the place is heaving. On Sunday mornings there's a good farmers' market.

A residential home inside the ghetto before sitting abandoned for years, Szimpla showcases the innovative spirit of the inner VII District, and its propensity to recycle the spaces that have defined its past.

Food and Drink

❶ KONYHA

Madách Imre út 8; tel: 1 322 5274; www.facebook.com/Konyha.Budapest; Tue–Thu noon–11pm, Fri–Sat noon–midnight, Sun noon–6pm; €€

Konyha offers a selection of imaginative dishes made with fresh, seasonal ingredients. Despite the high quality of the food, Konyha is a laid-back, trendy restaurant with no dress code, and a cosy and modern feel. Pets are welcome.

❷ VINTAGE GARDEN

Dob utca 21; tel: 30 790 6619; http://vintagegarden.hu/en; daily 9am–midnight; €€
This shabby-chic bistro has a Provençal feel, while still fusing some Hungarian accents into its dishes. You'll find French-bistro classics like *moules marinière* alongside Hungarian *gulyás* soup, as well as gourmet burgers.

❸ FRÖHLICH KÓSER CUKRÁSZDA

Dob utca 22; tel: 1 266 1733; www.frohlich.hu; Mon–Fri 9am–5pm; €
This kosher patisserie offers a range of Hungarian and Jewish pastries, from *flódni*, a Jewish pastry with nuts and fruit, to *chanukkai* donuts – on top of the classic *dobos* cake and custard cakes. More than 60 years old, it's a classic café with a slice of nostalgia.

❹ KARAVAN

Kazinczy utca 18; www.facebook.com/streetfoodkaravan; Mon–Thu 11.30am–midnight; Fri–Sun until 2am; €
This street food court has something for everyone, from vegan delicacies to sausage stands and fried-cheese burgers. You can grab something to drink from the bar or some food from one of the trucks and eat anywhere outdoors.

Strolling along Andrássy Avenue

ANDRÁSSY AVENUE

Andrássy Avenue is a Unesco World Heritage Site and Budapest's very own Champs Élysées. This elegant avenue stretches from central Budapest around St Stephen's Basilica all the way up to Heroes' Square and City Park.

DISTANCE: 3km (1.8 miles)
TIME: A half day
START: Erzsébet tér
END: Heroes' Square
POINTS TO NOTE: You can take the Millennium Underground for parts of the walk if you want to take a breather.

Andrássy Avenue – 2.3km (1.4-miles) long – was inaugurated in 1896 as part of Budapest's millennial celebrations, commemorating the 1,000-year anniversary of the Magyar's arrival in the Carpathian Basin. The avenue can be neatly split into four parts.

The section between Erzsébet tér and Oktogon is lined with designer boutiques and grand neoclassical monuments, including Budapest's answer to Broadway. Between Oktogon and Kodály körönd, the busy thoroughfare opens up and islands create a tree-lined walkway for pedestrians. From Kodály körönd until Bajza utca, Andrássy becomes more residential – with several palaces. The final part, reaching up to Heroes' Square, is home to villas containing a number of embassies, earning its fitting nickname, the Diplomatic Quarter (Diplomatanegyed).

One of the most important sights along Andrássy is actually underneath it: the Millennium Underground line, which serves the whole length of the avenue.

ERZSÉBET TÉR TO OKTOGON

Start your walk on **Erzsébet tér ❶**, a curious open square that merges modern design with green space. It's a popular spot in the summer, when young people come to hang out, frequenting its cafés and outdoor terrace bars.

Make your way over to Andrássy Avenue (Andrássy út), crossing Bajcsy-Zsilinszky út on the way. At the beginning of the boulevard, you'll find some wonderful examples of neo-Renaissance architecture. You'll also pass one of the entrances to the **Millennium Underground ❷**. Even if you don't plan to take it for part of the journey, it's worth going down to the platform to take a peek. You

Stunning ceiling decoration at the Hungarian State Opera House

can either go one stop to the Hungarian State Opera House (make sure you validate your ticket if you don't have a pass), or walk up Andrássy on foot.

Hungarian State Opera House

The spectacular **Hungarian State Opera House** ❸ (Magyar Állami Operaház; www.opera.hu; daily 10am–8pm; undergoing renovation, set to reopen in 2021), constructed by Miklós Ybl, one of Hungary's greatest architects in the late 19th century, opened in 1884. It is built in neo-Renaissance style, with arched colonnades and a dramatic romanticism captured in elements

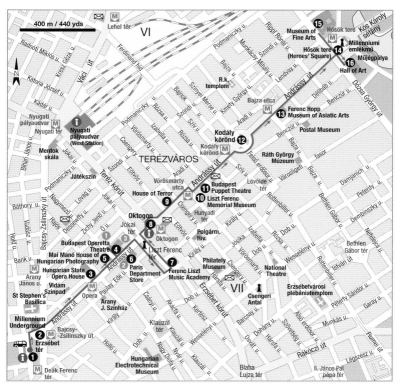

Budapest Operetta Theatre

like its sphinxes that pose majestically beside the grand entrance. A large balcony opens up above it, often used during private events and intervals.

The interior is decorated with frescoes, gold leaf and gilded mirrors. While its auditorium can only seat 1,300, its acoustics are among the best in Europe. If you are unable to catch a show, join a daily tour at 2, 3 or 4pm (tours will continue throughout the restoration works).

Budapest's Broadway

Nagymező utca, nicknamed 'Budapest's Broadway', runs perpendicular to Andrássy Avenue – take the second left after the Hungarian State Opera House. Somewhat unsurprisingly, you'll find a number of theatres located in close proximity.

The most notable is the **Budapest Operetta Theatre** ❹ (Budapesti Operettszínház; www.operett.hu), built in 1894 by Fellner and Helmer, an architect duo from Vienna. Up until World War I the building was home to an Orpheum bar, which reopened in 1923 as the Metropolitan Operetta Theatre, marking the beginning of the 'silver operetta' age. Since then, it's become the heart of the Hungarian Operetta tradition, featuring some of the most important actors and singers of the genre. With 500 performances and 400,000 guests a year, it's one of Hungary's most popular theatres.

Just opposite is the Thália Theatre, as well as the Radnóti Theatre on the other

side of Nagymező (across Andrássy Avenue). You'll also find the **Mai Manó House of Hungarian Photography** ❺ (Mai Manó Magyar Fotográfusok Háza; www.maimano.hu; Tue–Sun noon–7pm). The building is worth stopping to look at, with its large windows, elaborate frescoes and architectural detail. Don't skip the museum if you're at all interested in photography.

There's also a good number of cafés and restaurants, from elegant establishments to trendy street food vendors. For the latter, check out **Pizzica**, see ❶, for a great slice of pizza.

Head back onto Andrássy Avenue and keep an eye out for the former and legendary **Paris Department Store** ❻ (Párizsi Nagy Áruház). This former department store opened in 1911 and shows elements of Art Nouveau and Art Deco in its angular lines and elegant curves. If you want to stop for a drink with a view, take the lift on the side and head up to the top floor for **360 Bar**, see ❷. Alternatively, pop into **Kantin**, see ❸, for some modern Hungarian food.

Ferenc Liszt Music Academy

Turn into Liszt Ferenc tér on the right and continue down to the **Ferenc Liszt Music Academy** ❼ (Liszt Ferenc Zeneakadémia; https://lfze.hu; guided tours daily 1.30pm, ticket office daily 10am–6pm). Established in 1875, the academy was founded by its namesake composer – although it was originally located in the Liszt's former home

Mai Manó House

Emotive memorial at the House of Terror

near the Danube. This famous academy boasts an illustrious list of alumni, including Béla Bartók and Georg Solti.

The building itself is an exquisite piece of Art Nouveau architecture influenced by Vienna's Secessionists, created by Flóris Korb and Kálmán Giergl at the turn of the 20th century. Above the door, you'll see a statue of Ferenc Liszt himself. While the exterior is worth admiring, if you can, take one of the tours to explore inside. Its opulent interior features glazed Zsolnay tiles and incredible stained glass by Miksa Róth. Alternatively, take advantage of the regular performances held in its concert hall or music conservatory.

After you've had your musical fill, head back to Andrássy Avenue for the next section of the walk.

OKTOGON TO KODÁLY KÖRÖND

This busy intersection – where Andrássy Avenue and the Grand Boulevard cross – takes its name from its octagonal shape. Cross **Oktogon** ❽ so you end up on the left-hand side of Andrássy and continue straight up until you reach the House of Terror.

House of Terror
Number 60 on Andrássy Avenue is a rather intimidating building, topped with a metallic band with the word 'Terror' cut out to expose the sky. The **House of Terror** ❾ (Terror Háza; www.terror haza.hu; daily 10am–6pm) was once

the headquarters of the fascist Arrow Cross Party (supported by the Nazis); then, when the communists took over, the ÁVH (the secret police, similar to the KGB) established their headquarters in the very same building. Today it's a poignant museum commemorating those who were held captive, tortured and killed in the House of Terror, as well as the victims of the fascist and communist regimes in Hungary more widely.

The museum offers an interactive look into the history of Hungary in the mid-20th century, exploring the country's relationship with Nazi Germany and the Soviet Union, as well as looking at home-grown versions of these regimes.

The fact that the building was used by the Arrow Cross and the ÁVH makes the exhibits – and especially the commemorative installations – particularly moving. People were detained, interrogated, tortured and killed here: the basement reveals the cells in which victims were held, and a narrative in the lift describes the different methods of execution.

Liszt Ferenc Memorial Museum
For something a bit lighter, cross the road at Vörösmarty utca. On the corner with Andrássy Avenue is the **Liszt Ferenc Memorial Museum** ❿ (Liszt Ferenc Emlékmúzeum; www.lisztmu seum.hu; Mon–Fri 10am–6pm, Sat 9am–5pm). This small museum is a reconstruction of Liszt's last flat on the first floor of the original Academy of Music, where he lived between 1881

Iconic Heroes' Square

and 1886. In the collection, you'll find original instruments, books, scores, furniture, personal items and memorabilia. There is also a research centre.

Budapest Puppet Theatre

Further up Andrássy you'll come to the **Budapest Puppet Theatre ⓫** (Budapest Bábszínház; https://budapest babszinhaz.hu), one of the largest puppet theatres in Central Europe. Its shows – targeted at adults as much as children – showcase puppet theatre as a diverse and artistic genre rather than as a child-focussed activity. The theatre itself is located in a beautiful historic building dating from 1870, which has been home to various cabarets and even the National Theatre's Chamber Theatre. The professional puppet theatre opened in 1949. In the 1960s, the theatre became a focus of the international art scene, with its avant-garde shows 'choreographed' to classical music. Today, it's a local venue that caters to Budapest's residents, but the theatre has garnered an international reputation for its art.

KODÁLY KÖRÖND TO HEROES' SQUARE

Continue up until you reach **Kodály körönd ⓬**, a circus that lies at the intersection of Andrássy Avenue, Szinyei Merse utca and Felsőerdősor utca. While it is made up mostly of residential buildings, it's worth stopping to look at the façades. The four buildings, which form a full circle on the square, are accented with frescoes and neoclassical details, and you'll find bronze statues of Hungary's great heroes on the corners. The intersection was originally known just as Körönd (circus), before becoming Hitler Adolf tér between 1938 and 1945. It took its current name in 1971 to commemorate composer Zoltán Kodály, who lived in one of the buildings.

Beyond Kodály körönd, Andrássy Avenue opens up and becomes lined with villas. You should already have a good view of Heroes' Square from here.

Ferenc Hopp Museum of Asiatic Arts

Continue down to the **Ferenc Hopp Museum of Asiatic Arts ⓭** (Hopp Ferenc Kelet-Ázsiai Művészeti Múzeum; http://hoppmuseum.hu; Tue–Sun 10am–6pm). The museum, housed in a villa once belonging to Ferenc Hopp, was founded in 1919 to showcase art from East Asia. The collections are temporary, and can range from Japanese block prints to Chinese porcelains and Indonesian shadow puppets. The garden is inspired by Asian art, with a mix of Chinese, Japanese and Indonesian influences.

Heroes' Square

To get to Heroes' Square you can either walk the rest of the route or hop on the metro. Walking will allow you to take in some wonderful villas, ranging from neoclassical to Art Nouveau. Most of these house embassies, which is why this section of Andrássy Avenue has

Budapest Puppet Theatre   *Museum of Fine Arts*

earned the nickname the Diplomatanegyed (Diplomatic Quarter).

Heroes' Square ⑭ (Hősök tere) is one of Budapest's most famous squares. In the centre is a monument and a pedestrian area. In the backdrop you'll see the City Park, and on either side are neoclassical buildings, one housing the recently renovated **Museum of Fine Arts** ⑮ (Szépművészeti Múzeum; www. mfab.hu; Tue–Sun 10am–6pm) and the other the **Hall of Art** ⑯ (Műcsarnok; www.mucsarnok.hu; Tue–Wed and Fri–Sun 10am–6pm, Thu noon–8pm). The Hall of Art hosts regular exhibitions with a focus on contemporary art from Hungary and further afield.

The square is symbolic and home to the **Millenary Monument** (Ezeréves emlékmű), with a 36-metre (118ft) -high column topped by Archangel Gabriel. At its base, bronze sculptures of chieftains from the seven Magyar tribes who settled the Carpathian Basin surround the pillar. The memorial is also encircled by two curved colonnades featuring 14 statues representing some of Hungary's most emblematic historical figures. The monument was built for the millennial celebrations of 1896 to commemorate 1,000 years since the Magyars arrived.

At the base of the monument lies the 'Tomb of the Unknown Soldier', which – despite its name – is not a place of burial, but rather a cenotaph dedicated 'To the memory of the heroes who gave their lives for the freedom of our people and our national independence'.

Food and Drink

❶ PIZZICA

Nagymező utca 21; tel: 30 993 5481; www. facebook.com/pizzicapizza; Mon–Thu 11am–midnight, Fri-Sat until 3am; €

For quality street food on the go, pop into Pizzica. Run by an Italian, this is one of the best pizza places in the city. Thin-crusted pizzas are capped with buffalo mozzarella or truffle oil, with plenty of toppings to choose from.

❷ 360 BAR

Andrássy út 39; tel: 30 356 3047; www.360bar.hu; Mon–Wed 2pm-midnight, Thu–Sat 2pm–2am, Sun 2pm–midnight; €€
Set on the rooftop of the Paris Department Store, you can sip a cocktail or grab a bite while enjoying views that pan across the whole of Budapest.

❸ KANTIN

Andrássy út 44; tel: 20 280 7411; http:// kantinbudapest.hu; daily noon–midnight; €€
This modern Hungarian restaurant offers a three-course set menu. You can choose your starter from a selection of Hungarian delicacies, such as slices of salami or local goat's cheese, with mains including classics such as paprika chicken alongside more modern dishes.

City Park

CITY PARK AND AROUND

City Park is Budapest's much-loved green lung. With the romantic Vajdahunyad Castle, whose surrounding lake becomes an ice rink in the winter, and the famous Széchenyi Thermal Baths, it's the best place in the city to come to relax.

DISTANCE: 3.5km (2.2 miles)
TIME: A half day
START: Heroes' Square
END: Hungarian Geological and Geophysical Institute
POINTS TO NOTE: City Park is currently undergoing development to become a museum quarter, so parts of the park may be under construction. The main sites should be unchanged.

Located between Heroes' Square and the residential neighbourhood of Zugló, City Park (Városliget) is a welcome green oasis near the city centre. The park has a historical pedigree of its own – it was once called Ökördűlő, which translates as 'Oxmeadow', first mentioned in the mid-13th century under the archaic name Ukurföld. Its name changed frequently thereafter until Városliget was officially accepted. Városliget was one of the first public parks in the world.

Start at **Heroes' Square ①** (see page 58). Facing the park, take the road on the left round the side of the Museum of Fine Arts. Passing around the lake you'll find plenty of restaurants, such as the famous **Gundel**, see ①, or the more modest **Bagolyvár**, see ②. Continue on to reach the zoo.

AROUND THE ZOO

The entrance to **Budapest Zoo & Botanical Garden ②** (Fővárosi Állat- és Növénykert; www.zoobudapest.com; open daily, see website for seasonal times) is designed in Art Nouveau style, adorned with a troupe of elephants and a ring of polar bears. Inside the zoo, there are a number of exquisite Art Nouveau buildings, such as the famous elephant house, as well as more than 1,000 animal and 3,500 plant species to be seen. It's an interactive zoo and in some houses marsupials or birds may cross your path among the vegetation of their native habitat. It ranks among the oldest zoos in the world.

Leaving the zoo, continue down the road towards the Széchenyi Baths, which you'll find opposite the circus.

Széchenyi Thermal Bath   *Cooling off at Széchenyi in summer*

THE SZÉCHENYI THERMAL BATH

The **Széchenyi Thermal Bath** ❸ (Széchenyi gyógyfürdő; www.szechenyibath.hu; daily 6am–10pm) is one of the largest medicinal baths in Europe. The extensive complex has 11 indoor thermal water pools, one outdoor thermal pool, a number of immersion pools, a swimming pool and an activity pool, as well as saunas, massage rooms and treatment rooms. But it's the spectacular outdoor pools that really draw in the crowds. The building's canary-yellow exterior – in neo-Baroque style with elegant columns – makes a spectacular backdrop for visitors.

The bath is supplied by two thermal springs with temperatures of 74°C (165°F) and 77°C (170°F) respectively, which come with a thermal mineral pro-

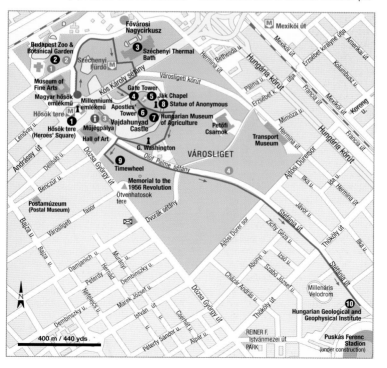

Vajdahunyad Castle Gate Tower

file including calcium, sulphate, bicarbonate and magnesium, as well as fluoride acid and metaboric acid. The water is said to help those suffering from medical conditions such as degenerative joint conditions and subacute joint inflammations.

While you'll find most of the city's thermal springs in Buda, close to the sources in the Buda Hills, this famous thermal bath over in Pest has mining engineer Vilmos Zsigmondy to thank, who conducted deep borings in City Park in the 19th century. In 1881, the predecessor of today's bath was already in operation; the Széchenyi Thermal Bath was built and expanded on the site of the original in 1913. It underwent further expansion in 1927 to create the outdoor pools and in 1960 to add the outpatient hospital.

Today, the baths come with state-of-the-art equipment, including a whirling corridor in the activity pool, along with underwater effervescence, a neck shower and water-beam back massage. In summer, Saturday nights see the outdoor pools host wild parties, complete with DJs, bars and spectacular lighting.

VAJDAHUNYAD CASTLE

From the Széchenyi Baths, cut across the park towards **Vajdahunyad Castle**. It was designed to catalogue 1,000 years of Hungarian architecture as part of the Millennium Exhibition in 1896. The castle was intended to be a temporary wooden construction, but proved so popular that it was rebuilt in brick and stone in 1908.

The Gate Tower

The castle is situated on Széchenyi Island at the heart of the park. The main entrance lies across a stone bridge topped with the **Gate Tower** ❹ (Kaputorony; www.mezogazdasagimuzeum.hu; daily 10am–7pm, tours every hour), an impressive twin-turreted structure overlooking the City Park lake. You can join a tour up to the top for a walk along the battlements and to enjoy a bird's eye view over the park and the castle grounds. Take in the details and curiosities of the castle, such as the rose window by Miksa Róth.

Ják Chapel

After crossing the Gate Tower, you'll see the **Ják Chapel** ❺ (Jáki kápolna; http://jakikapolna.hu; Mon, Wed, Fri 10am–1pm, 4–6pm) in the castle precinct on your left. The chapel is built in the earliest style incorporated into the castle complex (Romanesque – popular during the 11th–13th centuries). It's a reconstruction of the basilica in a 13th-century Benedictine monastery in the village of Ják, close to the Austrian border. Even if the visiting hours mean you can't go inside, peek into the cloisters and admire the elaborate carved portal at the entrance.

Apostle's Tower

Opposite the Ják Chapel, you'll see the **Apostles' Tower** ❻ (Apostolok tornya; www.mezogazdasagimuzeum.hu; Tue–Sun 10am–5pm, tours every hour), which was inspired by the clock tower in Sighisoara in Transylvania. It's quite a hike

Ják Chapel   *The popular statue of Anonymous*

up the 150 steps, but you are rewarded with a wonderful panorama of the city.

Hungarian Museum of Agriculture
Inside the castle proper is the **Hungarian Museum of Agriculture** ❼ (Magyar Mezőgazdasági Múzeum; www.mezogazdasagimuzeum.hu; Tue–Sun 10am–5pm). The building embraces the Baroque style inspired by Austrian palaces in the Austro-Hungarian Empire. The museum itself – more than 100 years old and survivor of two world wars – showcases Hungary's agricultural history, with a focus on forestry, hunting, viticulture and fishing. It also touches on Hungarian flora and fauna, as well as horse breeding.

Statue of Anonymous
Opposite the museum you'll see the bronze, seated, hooded Statue of **Anonymous** ❽. This sculpture by Miklós Ligeti depicts an 'unknown chronicler' of the Magyars, attributed with the first written account of Hungarian history, the *Gesta Hungarorum*, and whose only signature designated him as Master P (or P. dictus magister). One suggestion is that this mysterious figure was a 12th-century clerk in King Béla III's court. The shiny pen held in his hand is supposed to inspire writers, both practising and aspiring, should you touch it.

CITY PARK AND BEYOND

Exit the castle and follow the lake back towards Heroes' Square. You can grab a coffee or a meal with a castle view at the **Városliget Café & Restaurant**, see ❸, or continue away from the lake along Olof Palme. Stop and look at the **Timewheel** ❾ (Időkerék) nearby. This installation is a giant concave wheel that acts as one of the largest hour glasses in the world. Its particles are tiny pieces of glass that trickle through, with a computerised system to keep the timing perfect. Each New Year, the Timewheel is reset.

The Hungarian Gaudí

Born in 1845, Ödön Lechner is one of Hungary's greatest and most distinctive architects. The father of Hungarian Art Nouveau – known as Szecesszió – is sometimes dubbed as the Hungarian Gaudí for his use of colourful tiles and organic, nature-inspired motifs; however Lechner's work slightly predates his Catalan counterpart. Lechner's architecture is easy to recognise by his use of decorative tiles and ceramics from the Zsolnay factory in Pécs. His style is also unique in its search for a 'Hungarian language of form', merging Hungarian folk art with Orientalism, pursuing the Eastern heritage of the Magyar tribes, who were said to have come from Asia. His most famous buildings in Budapest are the Museum of Applied Arts (1896; see page 69), the Institute of Geology and Geophysics (1899) and the former Royal Postal Savings Bank (1901; see page 40).

Blue roof tiling on the Hungarian Geological and Geophysical Institute building

Along Olof Palme sétány, you'll pass **Kertem**, see ④, an outdoors bar and café that makes the perfect spot for a drink. You can either end your walk here, or – if you're interested in architecture – continue onto Stefánia út past the historic and residential villas to the Hungarian Geological and Geophysical Institute Building.

Hungarian Geological and Geophysical Institute building

Topped with blue tiles to represent the Tethys Ocean, with figures of Atlas on the rooftop holding up globes, this building by Ödön Lechner is one of the most spectacular by the 'Hungarian Gaudí'. The **Hungarian Geological and Geophysical Institute** ⑩ (Magyar Földtani és Geofizikai Intézet; generally visits by appointment only) opened in 1899 and combines Hungarian folk art with geological elements. It exemplifies Lechner's distinct Hungarian Art Nouveau style, particularly with the use of weather-resistant glazed Zsolnay tiles. The institute is home to an impressive collection of minerals that can be visited, along with the spectacular interior of the institute, for free (by appointment).

Food & Drink

① GUNDEL
Gundel Károly ut 4; tel: 1 889 8111; www.gundel.hu; Mon–Thu noon–11pm, Fri–Sat noon–midnight, Sun 11.30am–3pm and 7–11pm; €€€
One of Budapest's most famous restaurants due to its founding father Károly Gundel, who refined Hungarian cuisine and brought it into the world of haute cuisine. This elegant establishment has hosted a distinguished guest list of royals, politicians and celebrities.

② BAGOLYVÁR
Gundel Károly ut 4; tel: 1 889 8111; www.bagolyvar.com; daily noon–10pm; €€
Opened by Károly Gundel in 1913, this family-style restaurant was designed for zoo visitors. You can find traditional Hungarian dishes with that home-cooked feel and daily lunch menus that come at a set price.

③ VÁROSLIGET CAFÉ & RESTAURANT
Olof Palme stny 5; tel: 30 869 1426; www.varosligetcafe.hu; noon–10pm; €€
A fusion of traditional Hungarian and Austrian dishes with a modern twist. Located on the upper floor of the 19th-century ice-rink building with romantic views over to Vajdahunyad Castle and the City Park lake.

④ KERTEM
Olof Palme stny 2; tel: 70 202 7484; daily 11am–4am; €
Set on the terrace of the impressive red-bricked Olof Palme House in the heart of the park, this outdoor venue is a popular bar and chill-out place by day, with a festive feel at night.

The Italian Cultural Institute

THE PALACE DISTRICT

Located inside the Grand Boulevard, this part of the VIII District is characterised by elegant palatial apartments and leafy squares. Once a literary hub for classic writers, today the Palace District is known for its café culture and beautiful buildings.

DISTANCE: 2.5km (1.5 miles)
TIME: A half day
START: Ervin Szabó Library
END: Museum of Applied Arts
POINTS TO NOTE: Avoid doing this walk on a Monday, when the museums are closed.

Despite its name, the Palace District (Palotanegyed) has nothing to do with the Castle District across the river. After the great flood of 1838 destroyed most of the buildings in central Pest, much of the area underwent extensive reconstruction.

The Hungarian National Museum was completed here in 1847, and until the Hungarian Parliament building opened its doors in 1904, the Hungarian government operated from the National Museum and today's Italian Cultural Institute at Bródy Sándor utca 8. The museum's construction drew the city's elite, who built their palaces in the immediate vicinity.

Most of the Palace District's buildings were designed by the best archi-tects of the time, such as Miklós Ybl, who designed the Opera House and the Basilica. Between the 1860s and World War I, the main aristocratic fam-ilies and the mercantile elite erected more than 30 mansions in the area.

The area suffered widespread col-lateral damage during the two world wars and the 1956 uprising; you can still see bullet holes in some of the exteriors. Under the commu-nist regime, much of the area was neglected and dilapidated, and the entire VIII District – including the Pal-ace District – earned the reputation of being the poorest and most crime rid-den in Pest.

After the fall of communist rule in Hungary, the district's palaces were restored and investors turned their attention to the area. Today, it's a safe, green neighbourhood with grand mansions that now serve as cultural institutions or residential apartments. It's worth taking a look up now and then to appreciate the architectural details that make this area so special.

Ervin Szabó Library

AROUND THE ERVIN SZABÓ LIBRARY

Begin your walk at the start of Baross utca, outside the Ervin Szabó Library. You'll find plenty of cafés in this leafy square to choose from.

Ervin Szabó Library

This palatial building, located on the corner of Baross utca and Reviczky utca, houses the **Metropolitan Ervin Szabó Library** ❶ (Fővárosi Szabó Ervin könyvtár; www.fszek.hu; Mon–Fri 10am–8pm, Sat until 4pm, guided tours in English by appointment). It was built using the plans of Miklós Ybl – with accents from the Louis XV era in France – in 1867. This was not intended to be a library, but rather a palace for the Pálffy family, who resided in the bottom two levels while the top was rented out to students.

Almássy Palace

Turn down Ötpacsirta utca and you'll find the beautiful Almássy Palace. Today it's home to the **Hungarian Chamber of Architects** ❷ (Magyar Építészek Háza), but you can grab a coffee or a snack at the **Építész Pince**, see ❶, if you want to sit in the courtyard of this building and take it all in. Built in 1877 for Count Kálmán Almássy, the palace was designed by Antal Gottgeb. The front of the building is simple and elegant, but the garden and the courtyard are wonderfully romantic, lined with ivy-clad walls, with a wall fountain, sculptures and fanned yellow glass and iron above the entrance.

Count Alajos Károlyi Palace

Crossing Múzeum utca, **Count Alajos Károlyi Palace** ❸ (Gróf Károlyi Alajos Palota), by Miklós Ybl, has a collonaded entrance and striking

National Museum   *Textile exhibit, Hungarian National Museum*

neoclassical details. However, the story behind this palace – once belonging to the Károlyi family – is a tragic one. The aristocratic mansion burned down in 1945, and underwent several botched renovations, including a very ugly 1960s interior makeover. It's still only a shadow of its former self, and has no proper function, being deemed unsafe to enter.

Count Festetics Palace

Now an event venue and home to Andrássy University (Andrássy Egyetem), the **Festetics Palota** ❹ has fortunately been preserved both inside and out. The building boasts a neoclassical exterior, with Corinthian columns, and mirrored ballrooms and dazzling chandeliers inside.

Turn left on Bródy Sándor utca and head towards Múzeum körút. To get there, you'll pass the Italian Institute.

Outside the Festetics Palota

The Italian Cultural Institute

Once the Lower House of Representatives, designed by Miklós Ybl and completed in 1863, since the 1940s this palace has housed the **Italian Cultural Institute** ❺ (Olasz Kultúrintézet; www.iicbudapest.esteri.it; Mon and Thu 2–6pm, Tue–Wed 10am–1pm and 2–6pm, Fri 10am–1pm), incorporating a concert hall and a cinema, as well as a library.

Further on, on the corner with the Múzeum körút, you'll see the classic **Múzeum Kávéház és Étterem**, see ❷, to your right, and on the left, the Hungarian National Museum.

THE HUNGARIAN NATIONAL MUSEUM

Set in a leafy park, the **Hungarian National Museum** ❻ (Magyar Nemzeti Múzeum; https://mnm.hu; Tue–Sun 10am–6pm) is a white neoclassical wonder, with a romantic colonnade of Corinthian columns. The museum is the largest in Hungary and houses everything from the most important set of archaeological relics found around the Carpathian Basin to socialist memorabilia. The collection was founded by Count Ferenc Széchényi in 1802, who donated a generous selection of manuscripts, maps, coins and archaeological items. Today, the museum has eclectic displays ranging from prehistory to the Romans and the arrival of the Magyar tribes, with later exhibits including Ottoman artefacts, musical instruments and vintage photographs.

Beautiful stained-glass window at the Museum of Applied Arts

The Hungarian National Museum building has also played a crucial role in Hungarian history. On 15 March 1848, poet and revolutionary Sándor Petőfi gave an important speech on the steps of the museum – which was then the Upper House of the Hungarian Parliament – as part of the march that marked the beginning of the 1848–9 Revolution and War of Independence. Every year on 15 March, the museum plays a key part in the memorial celebrations.

BRÓDY SÁNDOR UTCA AND GUTENBERG TÉR

Exit the museum, return to Bródy Sándor utca and continue straight on.

The writer's district

The Palace District was traditionally not just a hangout for the aristocracy and bourgeoisie, but also attracted a literary crowd of Hungarian writers and poets. The area's most notable literary reference lies with *The Paul Street Boys* (*Pál Utcai Fiúk*) by Ferenc Móra, whose iconic children's book takes place here in the Palace District and its surroundings. Móra's title refers to a real street on the edge of the district – keep an eye out for it as you walk down Mária utca. Other writers and poets associated with the district include Sándor Bródy, who lived in the neighbourhood, and Gyula Krúdy, both of whom also have streets named after them.

Stop at numbers 5–7, which make up the **Former Hungarian Radio Headquarters** ❼ (Magyar Rádió). The building itself may look like the others on the street, but this was the starting point for another of Hungary's most important revolutions. On 23 October, the first shots of the Hungarian Revolution of 1956 were fired here – there's a memorial plaque outside the door, marking the spot.

Follow Bródy Sándor utca until you reach Gutenberg tér. This open square is worth a wander around, especially for views of the **Gutenberg Otthon Apartment House** ❽ (Edificio Gutenberg Muvelodési Otthon), which was once the property of the Hungarian Printers and Typesetters Benevolent Society. Built in 1906 by József and László Vágó, this block of apartments is a wonderful example of Art Nouveau, with its undulating façade and decorative ceramic details.

From Gutenberg tér, turn and continue straight down Mária utca. Turn right on Krúdy Gyula utca and continue until Mikszáth Kálmán tér.

MIKSZÁTH KÁLMAN TÉR AND SURROUNDINGS

Mikszáth Kálmán tér ❾ could pass for an Italian piazza. It's relaxed, has a mix of neo-Renaissance and neo-Gothic palatial apartments and is dotted with cafés and bars, such as **Lumen Kávézó**, see ❸.

Ödön Lechner's Museum of Applied Arts building

Next, head down Szentkirályi utca and up Baross utca until you reach Mária utca again. Turn right to reach Üllői út and head over to the Museums of Applied Arts.

Museum of Applied Arts

Before going into the **Museum of Applied Arts** ❿ (Iparművészeti Múzeum; www.imm.hu; at the time of writing, the museum was closed for renovation; see website for further details), take a moment to admire the building itself. One of the most famous of Ödön Lechner's works, it colours the street with its green and yellow rooftop made from Zsolnay tiles. The overall design mixes Indian and Iranian influences with Hungarian folk art; Lechner's intention was to create a branch of Hungarian Art Nouveau, drawing inspiration from the Magyars' supposed eastern roots. The Museum of Applied Arts is worth popping into for the architecture alone, with a fabulous stained-glass window above the entrance and Moorish arches encircling the main hall.

The museum has two permanent collections. The first includes furniture and artefacts from Hungarian and European traditions, while the other showcases a range of Islamic art and objects spanning 1,000 years.

Food and Drink

❶ ÉPÍTÉSZ PINCE

Ötpacsirta utca 2; tel: 1 266 4799; www.epiteszpince.hu; Mon–Thu 11am–10pm, Fri–Sat until 11pm; €

Építész Pince lies in the basement of the Chamber of Architects and serves Hungarian dishes at good prices. It's worth visiting for its impressive design and artsy crowd. If you can get a table in the beautiful courtyard, be sure to stop for a drink.

❷ MÚZEUM KÁVÉHÁZ ÉS ÉTTEREM

Múzeum krt. 12; tel: 1 267 0375; www.muzeumkavehaz.hu; Mon–Sat noon–3pm and 6pm–midnight, closed Sun and public holidays; €€

Capturing the feel of Budapest's Belle Epoque, this historic restaurant has been operating since 1885. While its decor is a throwback to another era, the menu offers a contemporary take on Hungarian cuisine.

❸ LUMEN KÁVÉZÓ

Mikszáth Kálmán tér 2; tel: 20 402 2393; www.lumenkave.hu; Mon–Fri 8am–midnight, Sat–Sun 10am–midnight; €

This modern café is one of the very few in Budapest to have its own roastery. If coffee's not your beat, you'll also find craft beers and local wines on the menu, along with soft drinks.

MARGARET ISLAND AND AROUND

Margaret Island is not just a green haven set in the middle of the Danube, it also comes with its own extensive history. Accessible by the Margaret and Árpád bridges, this car-free island is perfect if you're looking for a tranquil break from the city.

DISTANCE: 7km (4.5 miles)
TIME: A full day
START: Gül Baba's Tomb
END: Comedy Theatre of Budapest
POINTS TO NOTE: For tired legs – the island is rather long – return to Pest by bus.

When life in the city gets too chaotic, locals and visitors alike come to Margaret Island (Margitsziget) to escape for the day. Apart from the bus supplied by the city's public-transportation network (BKK, www.bkk. com), Margaret Island is completely free from traffic. You'll find swathes of leafy parkland across the whole 2.5km (1.5-mile) stretch of the island, encompassing flower-filled gardens, grassy picnic spots, cycle paths, medieval ruins, open-air theatres, wellness hotels and even a swimming-pool complex. And don't be surprised to see athletic types taking advantage of the 5km (3.1-mile) running track that traces the island's circumference.

Margaret Island is one of three islands that you'll find inside the city limits. The others are neighbouring Óbuda Island, and Csepel Island – to the south of Budapest – which is the largest island in Hungary. Óbuda and Margaret islands in particular have rich histories. It was the Romans who built the first villas and fortifications here (although nothing remains); then, in the 12th century, the knights of St John settled on the island.

Margaret Island was initially called Rabbit Island because the early Hungarian kings favoured it as a royal hunting reserve. Today's name originates from the time of King Béla IV and his daughter Margit. Following the Mongol invasion of 1241, King Béla IV pledged that should Hungary emerge safely from the attack, he would build a convent on the island and raise his daughter there as a nun. The island took her name in the 14th century, but Saint Margit was only canonised in 1943. Until the 16th-century Ottoman occupation when the Turks razed and destroyed its religious buildings, convents, churches and monasteries dominated the landscape of this green spot in the Danube.

Margaret Island and the blue Danube

Since the early 20th century, the island has been a public garden. As a result, the only buildings you'll find here are hotels, spas and restaurants.

But, before even setting foot on the island, you'll begin in Buda at one of the city's most unusual spots.

STARTING FROM BUDA

Budapest and a large part of Hungary lay under Ottoman rule for approximately 150 years. Apart from the Turkish thermal baths, not much has been left behind in the city from this period, although up on Rose Hill (Rózsadomb) you'll find **Gül Baba's Tomb ❶** (Gül Baba türbéje; Mon–Sun 10am–6pm). This tomb, built for a 16th-century dervish and personal companion of Suleiman the Magnificent, makes for a beautiful and surreal stop. Overlooking the Danube River, the octagonal-shaped tomb is surrounded by a rose garden, and displays some exquisite blue and white glazed Turkish tiles. Muslims revere Gül Baba as a saint, making his tomb the northernmost site of Islamic pilgrimage in existence today.

You can head down from the tomb to the river in two ways. Either descend via steep Gül Baba utca, which makes you think of a rural town in the hills with its historic houses and sloped, cobbled street, or via Mecset utca. If you opt for the former, you can pop into **Barako Kávéház**, see ❶, for a coffee on the aptly named Török utca (Turkish street). Next, make your way over to the bridge to take the pedestrian path halfway across it onto the island. (Make sure you keep to the left-hand side of the bridge.)

MARGARET ISLAND

Continue straight until you reach the **Centenary Monument ❷** (Centenáriumi emlékmû), an abstract metallic sculpture created in 1973 by István Kiss for the 100th anniversary of the unification of Buda, Pest and Óbuda. Nearby, you'll also pass the **Margaret Island Fountain ❸** (Margit Szigeti szökõkút), which comes to life in the late afternoon and early evening with a music and light show.

Ruins of the Franciscan Church and Monastery

Continue along the path in a straight line away from the fountain, passing through a shady park. The first of the ruins on Margaret Island you'll come across are those belonging to the 13th-century **Franciscan Church and Monastery ❹** (Ferences kolostor), which consists mainly of just a tower and a wall today. This former priory lies at the centre of the island and was likely built at the time of King Béla IV's rule. All the religious buildings were razed by the Ottomans when religious life ended abruptly, after which time Budapest's islands lay abandoned until the end of the 18th century when Palatine Archduke Joseph of Habsburg constructed a summer villa on this spot. It eventually became a hotel, but when that was damaged during World War

Water slides at Palatinus open-air baths

II and subsequently demolished, the Gothic ruins of the old Franciscan monastery resurfaced.

Margaret Island Mini Zoo

If you turn right after the Franciscan Monastery, you'll come across the **Margaret**

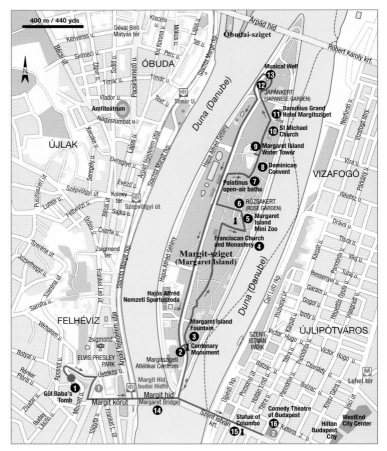

Island Mini Zoo ❺ (Margitszigeti kisállatkert; summer Mon–Fri 10am–6pm, weekends until 7pm), which is also called the Deer Park (Vadaspark). It has been operating on the island since 1950, before being incorporated into the Budapest Zoo and Botanical Garden group in 2002. You'll find a selection of wildlife, including deer and the island's (former) namesake rabbits, along with colourful birds like mandarin ducks and fluffy Asian silkies.

After the zoo, go left and inwards into the island. The perfumed **Rose Garden** ❻ (Rózsakert), which was created in 1927 and contains all types of roses, as well as the surrounding lawns and picnic areas, include some of the most beautiful spots on Margaret Island.

The Palatinus open-air baths

If you're looking to cool down a bit, head over to the **Palatinus open-air baths** ❼ (Palatinus strandfürdő; http://en.palatinusstrand.hu; daily 8am–8pm). While Budapest's bathing culture can be traced as far back as the Romans and perhaps even before that, the first open-air baths in the city, the Palatinus open-air baths, began life as a simple Danube beach in 1919.

A couple of years later, the beach was expanded to include a lido – the first large pool – but it was only when the baths were enlarged in 1937 that the Palatinus baths really came into their own.

Thermal springs run under the island and offer a natural supply of water for the pools. Over the decades, the baths have continued to grow and there are a total of nine today. They include a wave pool, thermal pools, a Marguerite pool, children's pools, and several swimming pools, including a 'fun pool', 'beach pool' and 'slide pool'.

The surrounding greenery of the island, coupled with its water quality, has made this a popular summer spot, but since renovation, parts of the complex (including a wellness section) are open year-round.

The ruins of the Dominican Convent

Head away from the Palatinus baths towards the right-hand side of the island, to the ruins of the **Dominican Convent** ❽ (Domonkos rendi apácakolostor). Built in the 13th century by King Béla IV, this former convent was also home to the king's daughter, Margit. After promising to commit his daughter to a life of pious devotion after defeating the Mongols, Margit was sent to the convent at the age of nine, and was canonised in 1943. Take a walk around these medieval ruins and keep an eye out for St Margit's sepulchre, a red marble tomb covered by a wrought-iron grille. You can also take in the ruins from a viewing point erected just above the convent. If you look north, you can probably see the water tower already peeking up above the trees.

The Margaret Island Water Tower

The **Margaret Island Water Tower** ❾ (Margitszigeti víztorony), the symbol

Japanese Garden

of the island itself, is a spectacular Art Nouveau structure built in 1911 by Rezső Vilmos Ray, with collaboration from Dr Szilárd Zielinski, a professor from the Technical University. This 66-metre (217ft) -high water tower was a revolutionary building at the time, as it was one of the first ferro-concrete buildings in Europe and it also provided the island with an undisturbed water supply. A feat of engineering, the water tower has become an iconic part of the Budapest cityscape.

Immediately beneath the tower, you'll find the **Margaret Island Open-air Theatre** (Margitsziget szabadtéri színpad; http://eng.szabadter.hu; ticket office Mon noon–6pm, Tue–Fri 10am–6pm), which has operated on the grounds since 2011 and is one of the main venues for the Budapest Summer Festival.

The Saint Michael Church
The reconstructed **St Michael Church** ⑩ (Szent Mihály kápolna), a 12th-century Romanesque Premonstratensian Church, lies close to the base of the water tower. The original church was probably destroyed – like the other religious buildings – during the Ottoman occupation. The current church is a 1930s replica and is still in operation. The bell in the tower, however, dates back to the 15th century and has a mysterious backstory, having been discovered under the roots of an overturned walnut tree following a storm in 1914. Some believe monks buried the bell when the Turks invaded.

Keep an eye out for the Artists' Promenade (Művész-sétány), where you'll find statues and busts of famous Hungarian composers, artists, sculptors, poets and writers.

Heading north, you'll pass the **Danubius Grand Hotel Margitsziget** ⑪ for a turn-of-the-century feel. Built by Miklós Ybl, the architect behind the Hungarian State Opera House (among other landmarks), the hotel is worth stopping to look at.

The Japanese Garden
To the north of the island, the **Japanese Garden** ⑫ (Japánkert) is perhaps the island's most beautiful spot, with lilies and koi carp swimming in its maple-shaded pond, set alongside bamboo groves, a small curved wooden bridge and even a waterfall. The garden was initially created in the 1970s, but had been neglected until recent years, when the garden underwent a full renovation. New plants came in to enrich the grounds, and accents were added to give the garden a more Japanese feel. It's a popular place on the island to relax and while away the day.

The Musical Well
Just after the Japanese Garden, you'll find a gazebo with drinking fountains to the side. This **Musical Well** ⑬ (Zenélő kút) is a replica of another fountain in Transylvania and gets its name for playing children's songs in the morning and afternoon throughout the summer. It's also a popular spot for concerts in the summer months.

Margaret Bridge　　　　　　*Family fun on Margaret Island*

From here you can walk back across the island towards Margaret Bridge to return to the city centre, or you can take the 26 or 226 bus back into town or part of the way. For a scenic walk back into town, get off at the stop marked 'Margitsziget/Margít Híd' and cross the bridge on foot. At the centre of the bridge you'll have stunning views over the city, with Buda Castle and the Hungarian Parliament building in the distance.

Margaret Bridge ⓮ (Margit Híd) is a beautiful landmark in its own right. This three-way bridge was built by French engineer Ernest Goüin in the 1870s, and was the second permanent bridge in the city after the Széchenyi Chain Bridge.

ENDING IN PEST

Crossing the bridge, you'll come out onto Jászai Mari tér and the start of the Grand Boulevard (Nagykörút/Szent István körút) on the Pest side of the river. If you continue down on the left-hand side, you'll pass Falk Miksa utca and a curious bronze **statue of Columbo** ⓯, scratching his head at the sight of a bronze dog. Some believe there is a connection between the Colombo actor Peter Falk, who has Hungarian roots, and the name of the street. One urban legend is that Peter Falk was related to the Miksa Falk family, but the connection has never been proven.

Further down the street you'll reach the final landmark on this walk, the **Comedy Theatre of Budapest** ⓰ (Vígszín-

ház; www.vigszinhaz.hu), with its curved façade and neoclassical elements. The theatre – one of the oldest operational theatres in Budapest – was completed in 1896 by Fellner and Helmer, who built 'modern' theatres all across Central Europe. It became a hub for modern acting, putting on international work from French comedies to Chekhov and Shakespeare. Today, it remains an important cultural institution.

If the walk has inspired an appetite, you can pop into **Kino Cafe Mozi**, see ❷, next door, for a drink or a light snack.

Food & Drink

❶ BARAKO KÁVÉHÁZ

Török utca 3; tel: 30 283 7065; Mon–Fri 9am–7pm, Sat–Sun until 6pm; €
This third-wave café offers unique coffees from Arabica beans and those made from rare Barako coffee from the Philippines. It's a small café, but worth a visit for those interested in trying new and unusual coffees. There's something here to suit everyone's taste – just ask for it!

❷ KINO CAFE MOZI

Szent István krt. 16; tel: 1 224 5650; http://kinocafemozi.hu; daily noon–8pm; €
Housing its own small art-house cinema, this unique café is popular with hip, young locals. You can get the usual sandwiches and salads you'd find in any café, but the bohemian atmosphere is the real draw.

The Great Market Hall

SOUTH PEST

Southern Pest was once an industrial area set close to the Danube, but after initiatives to rebuild and renovate its red-bricked factories into art and cultural centres, gastronomy and craft-beer hubs, it's become an exciting district to visit.

DISTANCE: 5km (3 miles)
TIME: A full day
START: Kálvin tér
END: Trafó House of Contemporary Arts
POINTS TO NOTE: This route ventures off the tourist track and offers more unusual sites to see in the city. It's advisable to take the tram for parts of it.

The IX District covers a large area that spans the southern side of the Danube. It also goes by the name of Francis Town (Ferencváros), which was originally developed in the 1700s. Being right on the Danube, much of the area experienced significant flooding in both the 18th and 19th centuries, after which time brick and stone buildings were constructed, designed to withstand any serious damage. In the second half of the 19th century, the district became an industrial hub, populated with mills, the largest slaughterhouse in Hungary and liquor and glass factories, as well as the beautiful Great Market Hall.

Today, the area has seen significant investment, with a whole new cultural quarter being constructed, and a lively café and restaurant scene on the mostly pedestrianised Ráday utca. Whereas until recently visitors only came here for the Great Market Hall, more and more people are coming to South Pest, looking for an edgier experience than that offered by many of the city's other central areas.

AROUND KÁLVIN TÉR AND THE DANUBE

Start your walk in **Kálvin tér ❶**. This square is the meeting point of three districts, where the old Inner City (V District) meets the Palace District (VIII District) and Ferencváros (IX District). The most notable landmark is the large Calvinist Church. If you want to grab lunch or a coffee, the start of Ráday utca on the corner of the square offers a number of choices.

Otherwise, take the boulevard in the direction of the Danube and continue straight on until you reach the Great Market Hall.

The Great Market Hall

The **Great Market Hall** ❷ (Nagyvásárcsarnok; www.piaconline.hu; Mon 6am–5pm, Tue–Fri until 6pm, Sat until 3pm) is Budapest's oldest and largest indoor market. Samu Pecz

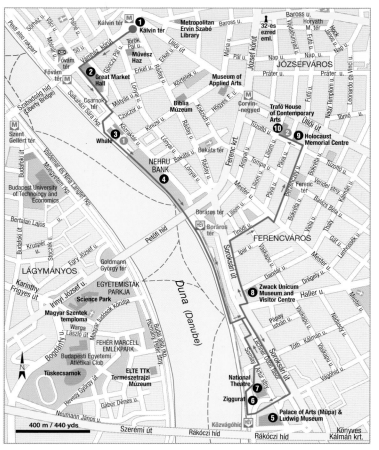

The Ludwig Museum

built and designed the market in around 1897, creating a grand neo-Gothic building that spans three floors with beautiful iron and steel work.

This is one of Budapest's most visited spots, and it's also a great place to pick up some Hungarian delicacies to take home, from Tokaji wine to paprika and tins of goose liver. You can also find fresh produce including seasonal fruit and vegetables, mushrooms, meat cuts, baked goods, cheeses and more. The first floor has Hungarian folk crafts for sale along with other souvenirs.

Exit the market on the opposite side from the main entrance and you'll see an interesting structure straight ahead made from brick and glass.

The Whale

This unique cultural and commercial centre is located within a 19th-century brick building topped with an undulating glass shell that curves into the shape of a whale – hence the name. The **Whale** ❸ (Bálna; www.balnabudapest.hu; Sun–Thu 10am–8pm, Fri–Sat until 10pm) is a gastro and design hub right on the banks of the Danube, and is also home to the Budapest Gallery. It's a refreshing place to stop for a beer with a view; try the terrace of the **Jónás Craft Beer House**, see ❶.

Next to the Whale is the green **Nehru Bank** ❹ (Nehru Part), with wonderful panoramas over Buda. Wander through the park or on the riverside

path to Petőfi Bridge (Petőfi híd). Under the bridge you can grab the number 2 tram, or if you time it right, take the public-transport boat, to the Müpa-Nemzeti Színház stop to explore the Millennial Cultural Centre.

THE MILLENNIAL QUARTER

The Millennial Cultural Centre (Millenniumi Kulturális Központ) began with the National Theatre (opened in 2002), followed shortly thereafter by the Palace of Arts in 2005. This entirely modern quarter serves as a cultural hub, combining art, music and theatre with modern architecture and design.

The Palace of Arts

As you get off the tram you'll see the **Palace of Arts** ❺ (Művészetek Palotája or Müpa for short; www.mupa.hu; daily 10am–6pm) to your right (and to your left if you come by boat). This cutting-edge angular building has won several architectural recognitions for its simplicity and design. It's home to a complex of halls, including the 1,525-seat Béla Bartók National Concert Hall. Regarded as one of the best auditoriums in Europe, the hall frequently features big names from the classical-music scene and world-renowned orchestras.

The Ludwig Museum

Located in the Palace of Arts building, the **Ludwig Museum** (Ludwig

The National Theatre and the spiral Ziggurat

Múzeum; www.ludwigmuseum.hu; Tue–Sun 10am–8pm) is a modern exhibition space spread across 3,300 sq metres (35,520 sq ft). While its collection boasts an impressive catalogue of American Pop Art, it also houses an extensive body of work by Hungarian and Central and Eastern European artists. You'll also find some fine temporary exhibitions.

The National Theatre

Opposite the Ludwig Museum is the National Theatre complex. Before heading over to the theatre, take a look at the curious **Ziggurat** ❻ in its gardens. This surreal building spiralling up by the Danube contains a gallery belonging to the National Theatre. You can also walk up the winding path to the top for wonderful views over the city, the theatre and the surrounding garden.

The **National Theatre** ❼ (Nemzeti Színház; https://nemzetiszinhaz.hu) itself is also a curious building, blending classical elements with modern architecture – check out the nine muses on the building's curved, glass-covered façade. It was designed by Mária Siklós and houses three venues.

The park in front of the theatre is full of curiosities, where a platform juts out into a pond to look like the bough of a ship. In the water, you can see a sculpture of a submerged Greek temple. One of the paths here leads to a sculpture of a gate draped with curtains by Miklós Melocco.

Next, wander along the path by the modern glass office and aparment blocks before turning right to Soroksári út.

THE REHABILITATED AREA

At the intersection with Haller utca, cross over to the Unicum Factory. This part of central Ferencváros is known for its ongoing redevelopment projects, and has been nicknamed the Rehabilitated Area (Rehabilitációs terület). Despite being mostly residential, there are some interesting places worth seeing, including the Zwack Unicum Factory.

The Zwack Unicum Museum and Visitor's Centre

Once the factory for Hungary's signature bitter liqueur, Unicum, this beautiful brick building has opened itself up to the public as a museum. The **Zwack Unicum Museum** ❽ (Zwack Unicum Múzeum és Látogatóközpont; https://unicum.hu; Mon–Sat 10am–5pm) offers visitors the chance to learn all about the mysterious 200-year-old Unicum, whose recipe of 40 herbs and spices remains a top secret guarded by the Zwack family. You can explore the cellars and try some interesting variations, as well as taking in some of Unicum's iconic advertising over the past century. And for something a little more offbeat, the museum also hosts the largest miniature bottle collection in Central Europe, with more than 17,000 pieces.

The Holocaust Memorial Centre garden

From the Unicum Factory, turn right down Soroksári út and walk to Tinódi utca. Here you'll see more signs of the area's industrial heritage, such as a former mill that has been turned into loft apartments. Turn down Tinódi and take a right at Mester utca. Head left at Berzenczey utca, past Ferenc tér, before taking another left at Tűzoltó utca. In Páva utca (the first street you'll come to) you'll see the Holocaust Memorial Centre.

Food & Drink

① JÓNÁS CRAFT BEER HOUSE

Fővám tér 11; tel: 70 930 1392; www. facebook.com/pg/jonaskezmuvessorhaz; Mon–Thu 11am–midnight, Fri–Sat until 2am, Sun closed; €€

Located in the Bálna, Jónás Craft Beer House has an attractive terrace with views over the river and a good selection of local craft beers. If you want something other than beer, you can get coffee, fresh lemonade or harder drinks – no coke though.

② ÉLESZTŐ

Tűzoltó utca 22; tel: 70 336 1279; www. elesztohaz.hu; daily 3pm–3am; €€

This craft-beer hub is set in a former glass works that is more than a bar. You'll find over 20 Hungarian craft beers on tap, plus you can also get imported beers, beer cocktails and snacks.

Holocaust Memorial Centre

The **Holocaust Memorial Centre** ❾ (Holokauszt Emlékközpont; www. hdke.hu/en; Tue–Sun 10am–6pm) is a memorial and museum dedicated to the Hungarian Jews and Roma killed during the Holocaust. The centre is situated in a former synagogue, which was renovated and opened as a museum in 2004. It combines the original design with modern, asymmetric architecture by István Mányi. The permanent collection focuses on the persecution, suffering and extermination of Hungary's Jews and Roma during World War II, as well as the wider relationship between citizen and state. You'll find illuminating temporary displays here as well.

Back on Tűzoltó utca, you'll pass **Élesztő**, see ❷, a craft-beer hub housed in a former glass factory, where you can stop and try a number of brews; alternatively, end the tour at Trafó.

Trafó

Trafó House of Contemporary Arts ❿ (Trafó Kortárs Művészetek Háza; http:// trafo.hu; show days 4–10pm) is set in a former transformer station. Today, it's a modern and avant-garde venue showcasing contemporary arts from theatre and dance to visual arts. You'll find artists performing here from Hungary and further afield, and there's also a gallery and a club. Stop for a show, or explore the bar scene in the area – nearby Tompa utca is a good place to start.

Castle Garden Bazaar

SOUTH BUDA

This part of southern Buda stretches down from the base of Castle Hill over to Gellért Hill and the trendy Bartók Béla Boulevard. It's known for its river views, thermal waters and café culture.

DISTANCE: 3km (1.8 miles)
TIME: A half day
START: Castle Garden Bazaar
END: Gárdonyi tér
POINTS TO NOTE: Much of this walk involves hiking up Gellért Hill, so make sure you wear some comfy shoes, and bring swimwear if you're interested in visiting the baths.

Encompassing three areas – Tabán, Gellért Hill and Bartók Béla út in districts I and XI – this part of Buda is slightly off the tourist trail when comparing it to the Palace District, but you'll still find plenty of views and sites to explore.

The area of Tabán lies behind the Royal Palace, consisting mostly of a green park with a few villas dotted around the edge. The area has been inhabited since Neolithic times, being a populous village in the Middle Ages thanks to its proximity to the castle. You may not believe it today, but up until the early 20th century you'd have found a bustling multicultural community here.

Tabán backs onto Gellért Hill, named for St Gellért, an 11th-century Italian monk martyred here after the pagans bundled him into a barrel and threw him down the hill.

On the other side, the area around Bartók Béla Boulevard is a mix of fin de siècle buildings and wonderful café culture.

TABÁN AND AROUND

Start at this impressive neo-Renaissance complex leading up to the castle. With a dramatic rampart of colonnades and viewing platforms, the **Castle Garden Bazaar ❶** (Várkert Bazaar) stretches along the Danube, accented with statues and fountains. It was initially built at the end of the 19th century by Miklós Ybl, but was left neglected for a long time, until 2014 renovations turned it into a cultural hub with exhibition halls, shops and a new park. Turn right into Apród utca, passing the Semmelweis Medical History Museum.

Walking up Gellért Hill

Semmelweis Medical History Museum
If you're interested in an alternative perspective on history, stop to visit the **Semmelweis Medical History Museum ❷** (Semmelweis Orvostörténeti Múzeum; http://semmelweismuseum.hu; Tue–Sun summer 10am–6pm, winter until 4pm). The museum's namesake, Ignác Semmelweis, was born in this street more than 200 years ago and earned his fame in the medical community for discovering the cause and cure for puerperal fever. The museum of medical history and its library have since taken up residence in Semmelweis' abode.

After the museum, turn down Attila út and you'll see a white catholic church with twin towers to your left, and across the road the green slopes of Tabán. Next to the church you can stop for a coffee and cake at **Asztalka Cukrászda**, see ❶, or continue towards Döbrentei tér park, underneath Elizabeth Bridge (Erzsébet híd).

In the middle of the park you'll see the **statue of Elizabeth ❸**, the Habsburg Empress better known as Sissi. She was the consort of Franz Josef and much loved by the Hungarian people, most particularly for her ability to speak Hungarian. The statue lies next to the entrance of an underpass –

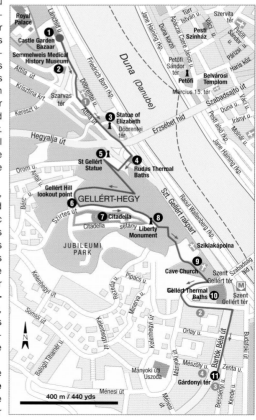

Rudas Thermal Baths *Citadella and the Liberty Monument*

follow the road through it and you'll arrive at the Rudas Baths.

The Rudas Thermal Baths

If you're curious to try one of the original Ottoman baths, head into the **Rudas Thermal Baths** ❹ (Rudas Gyögyfürdõ; www.rudasfurdo.hu; daily 6am-8pm, night bathing Fri−Sat 10pm−4am). However, it's important to note that the baths are single sex on weekdays – with women only allowed on Tuesdays and men allowed during the rest of the week – however, weekends are mixed.

This thermal bath has been in operation since 1520, and it follows the usual Turkish structure, with the main pinpricked dome covering the octagonal central pool, with four small pools at each corner.

You can extend your ticket to include the 19th-century swimming pool and the modern wellness centre, which includes a rooftop Jacuzzi with views across the river.

From the Rudas Baths, walk back up behind the dome of the old Turkish bath and cross the road to start your ascent up Gellért Hill.

GELLÉRT HILL

Locate the staircase leading up to the hill. It's impossible to miss, with a waterfall running down the middle in the summer months. Take the stairs up to the **St Gellért Statue** ❺ (Szent Gellért-szobor).

This monument was erected in 1904 on the spot where it's said that St Gellért met his end. The 12-metre (40ft) -tall bronze statue shows the saint proudly holding a cross above the city. At his feet, wild, pagan Magyars look up at the Venetian monk. Behind him is a curved colonnade.

Gellért Hill (Gellért-hegy) is a labyrinth of paths. Take the one up away from the statue that goes up towards the Citadella. Turn right, wander along the hill and then head up again. You should come to the **Gellért Hill lookout point** ❻ (Gellért-hegyi kilátó). From here, you will have one of the most beautiful views in the city, capturing the Castle, Parliament and the Chain Bridge in the distance. Behind, you'll see the Citadella walls – once you've taken in the vista, make your way to the old fortress.

Citadella and the Liberty Monument

The **Citadella** ❼ was originally built by the Habsburgs following the 1848−9 revolution, with the aim of intimidating the Hungarian population. Today, it's become a symbol of freedom, having become virtually obsolete by the time it was completed in 1954 – the political mood was already moving towards the conciliation of Austria and Hungary in 1967, and the citadel lost its military function. You can still admire its imposing structure and cannons. Round the back, the **Liberty Monument** ❽ (Szabadság szobor) towers over you, a 14-metre (46ft) pillar with a bronze

Marx and Engels Cubist statue, Memento Park

lady atop, holding a palm leaf above her head with both hands. The statue was initially a Soviet memorial, erected in 1947 to remember the Soviet soldiers who fell while taking the city from the Germans. However, in 1992, all Soviet elements were moved over to Memento Park (see box).

Take the steps down behind the Liberty Monument and follow the path to the Gellért Hill Cave Church.

Memento Park

If the bronze statues on top of Gellért Hill pique your interest, you may want to pay a visit to Memento Park (www.mementopark.hu; daily 10am–dusk). This open-air museum is where the statues erected under communist Hungary are located, out in the southern suburbs of Buda and accessible by the 150 bus from Újbuda-központ. The park was developed in the early 1990s as a home for some 42 monuments and plaques from the communist period, spanning 1949–89. They were removed from other parts of the city following the collapse of the Soviet Union, including the Red Army soldier statue that once belonged to the ensemble of the Liberty Monument on Gellért Hill. You can extend your visit to South Buda with a trip to this Social Realist Disneyland – simply continue from Gárdonyi tér on foot or by tram to Újbuda-központ and hop on the bus.

Gellért Hill Cave Church

St Ivan's Cave (Szent Iván barlang) belongs to a network of natural caves running under Gellért Hill. It takes its name from a 9th-century hermit who resided within the cavern, using the nearby water source (now used by the Gellért Baths) to heal people. The cave became a sacred place for the Order of St Paul in the 1920s. After visiting the grotto in Lourdes, this group of Hungarian Pauline monks converted the cave into a chapel; work began in 1926 and was completed in 1931, with the help of architect Kálmán Lux. The **Cave Church** ❾ (Sziklatemplom; www.sziklatemplom.hu; Mon–Sat 9.30am–7.30pm) incorporates the natural cave wall. Curiously, the temperature inside always hovering around 20 degrees due to the nearby thermal springs. You can visit any time, providing there is no mass going on.

The Gellért Thermal Baths

If you didn't get the chance to bathe at the Rudas, the **Gellért Thermal Baths** ❿ (Gellért Gyógyfürdő; www.gellertbath.hu; daily 6am–8pm) are worth visiting for the Art Nouveau architecture alone. The complex uses the thermal water from the hill, and is partitioned into indoor and outdoor pools. The indoor thermal baths are adorned with turquoise blue Zsolnay tiles and ceramics, whereas the main swimming pool lies under a glass rooftop and undulating columns. The outdoor pools were a later addition, and each hour you

Gellért Thermal Baths   *Inside the Cave Church*

can enjoy the eccentric wave machine – one of the first in Europe.

On your way out of the baths, head up the road to the top of Kemenes utca for a drink at **Pagony**, see ❷, a unique bar set in the former outdoor bathing complex. Afterwards, go downhill to Bartók Béla út.

BARTÓK BÉLA ÚT

This elegant avenue is lined with fine buildings, and you'll notice Art Nouveau details in some of the houses. The area has become trendy with its density of design shops, private galleries and hip cafés. At the end, you'll reach **Gárdonyi tér** ⓫, a beautiful square with a dramatic building enclosing **Hadik & Szatyor**, see ❸, a once well-known literary hub. This is a great place to relax – enjoy a coffee, slice of cake or dinner in **Hadik**, or a drink in its neighbouring bar, **Szatyor**. Alternatively, cross the road to **Kelet Kávezó és Galéria**, see ❹.

Food & Drink

❶ ASZTALKA CUKRÁSZDA
Döbrentei utca 15; tel: 20 581 3399; www.asztalkacukraszda.hu; Mon–Fri 11am–6pm, Sat–Sun until 7pm; €
This cosy café and cake shop has an outdoor terrace with views over Tabán and Gellért Hill, as well as an indoor section that feels like a dainty living room. You'll find an attractive selection of cakes here, with the usual offering of coffee and tea.

❷ PAGONY
Kemenes utca 10; tel: 31 783 6411; www.pagonykert.hu; Mon–Fri 9am–10pm, Sat–Sun 11am–10pm; €€
This is one of the most unique venues in Budapest. Set in the disused pools that once belonged to the outdoor part of the Gellért Thermal Baths, Pagony is a summer bistro where you can find cheese plates and craft burgers, as well as a tempting list of wines and beers.

❸ HADIK & SZATYOR
Bartók Béla út 36; tel: 1 279 0291; www.hadik.eu, www.szatyorbar.com, noon–1am; €€
This duo of bar (Szatyor) and restaurant (Hadik) may open up into each other under one roof, but have a different feel. Hadik has a clean, industrial air and was once a literary hangout for Hungarian writers, whereas Szatyor embraces the shabby-chic aesthetic of Budapest's ruin bars.

❹ KELET KÁVEZÓ ÉS GALÉRIA
Bartók Béla út 29; tel: 20 456 5507; www.facebook.com/keletkavezo; Mon–Fri 7.30am–11pm, Sat–Sun 9am–11pm; €€
This quirky café, lined with second-hand books, is popular for its wide selection of teas, third-wave coffees and tasty toasted sandwiches and curries.

BUDA HILLS

If you want to get out into nature, there is no need to leave the city limits.
The Buda Hills are popular for their hiking trails, residential areas filled
with beautiful villas and for the unique Children's Railway.

DISTANCE: 17km (10.5 miles)
TIME: A full day
START: Zugliget Chairlift
END: Hűvösvölgy
POINTS TO NOTE: This route
involves various modes of unusual
transportation, such as a chair lift,
cogwheel train and the Children's
Railway. However, expect a bit of
moderate hiking and walking as well.

While Pest is completely flat, Buda undulates along a curve of hills. Towards the western fringes of the city, the peaks can rise up to over 500 metres (1, 640ft). The Buda Hills (Budai-hegység) blur the boundary between where the city ends and the countryside begins, with a mix of residential areas that immediately back onto forests full of game and hiking spots. While each hill has its own name, it can be hard to tell where one hill stops and another begins.

The highest point of Budapest is János Hill (János-hegy), whose lookout tower can be seen in the far distance from most parts of the city. This route includes a bit of hiking, plus some relaxing sightseeing that won't require any walking.

The easiest way to get to the starting point is to take the 291 bus, which runs from Nyugati train station (Nyugati pályaudvar) to Zugliget, Libegő. From here, the route leads out into the Buda Hills.

JÁNOS-HEGY

At the base of János-hegy, you can either hike up the hard way or take the **Zugliget Chairlift** ❶ (Zugliget Libegő; https://www.bkv.hu/en/zugliget_chairlift_/; seasonal opening hours, see website) to the top. This cable-suspended chairlift is just over 1km (0.6-miles) long and takes about 15 minutes.

The chairlift will put you down right on the top of János-hegy. You'll find a café and some street food options if riding the cable car has whetted your appetite, but if you're itching to hike, head over to the Elisabeth Lookout Tower.

View over Budapest from the Buda Hills

Elisabeth Lookout

Right atop János-hegy, the **Elisabeth Lookout ❷** (Erzsébet kilátó) is a popular spot for locals and visitors alike. At 527 metres (1,729ft), this is the highest point inside the city limits, and when the weather conditions are right you can see parts of the Great Hungarian Plain as far as 80km (50 miles) away.

The tower was named after the beloved Empress 'Sissi', who loved walking in the hills, but this neo-medieval tower was actually built in 1911. If the style reminds you of Fisherman's Bastion on Castle Hill (see page 34), that's because the same architect, Frigyes Schulek, was behind the design. Go inside the tower and climb up the stone spiral staircase for staggering panoramic views. It's worth the hike simply to appreciate the Buda Hills from their highest point.

Descend the tower and walk back as if you were going to take the chair lift again, but instead follow the path towards Normafa. This wooded walkway takes you on a scenic trail that scales the top of the hill, bridging János-hegy and Svábhegy together.

SVÁBHEGY

The path will lead you to a clearing with excellent views down to the city – the Elizabeth Lookout now appears almost miniature in the distance. You'll likely see people barbecuing on the side of the hill, dogs running around and kids playing jubilantly. **Normafa ❸** is a popular spot

The Children's Railway in Hűvösvölgy

throughout the seasons, whether it's picnics and barbecues in summer or sledding in winter.

As the trail ends, you'll see the residential area around Normafa come into view. You can opt to take the bus for a few stops to **Svábhegy** ❹. Alternatively, continue on foot to explore this lesser-known part of Budapest. The walk is scenic, passing wrought-iron gates enclosing mysterious ivy-clad villas and their gardens, some of which are abandoned. Simply continue straight down Eötvös út until you reach a junction with Diana utca (this is also where the bus will drop you).

At the 'Svábhegy junction', you'll find a few places to eat and drink. For traditional southern Hungarian food (heavy on fish), you'll want to have lunch at **Bajai Halászcsárda**, see ❶. Or, if you're craving something sweet, head into the conservatory of **Szamos Szépkilátás Cukrászda**, see ❷, for a cake and a coffee.

Once you're done, cross over to the **cogwheel railway** ❺ (Fogaskerekű; www. bkk.hu; daily 5am–11pm) and board the train heading up to Széchényi-hegy.

Getting transportation up to the Buda Hills has been a priority since the 19th century. In 1868, a horse tramway was introduced, running from Chain Bridge to Zugliget at the base of János-hegy, prompting an initiative to construct another service up to Svábhegy. About five years later, Niklaus Riggenbach, the man behind Europe's first cogwheel railway in the Swiss Alps, received a permit to build another cogwheel railway up to

Svábhegy, which opened in 1874.

The line used Riggenbach's cogwheel system, which was built along a single-track railway covering a distance of almost 3km (1.9 miles), and up an elevation of 264 metres (866ft). The line was extended in 1890 to go up Széchenyi-hegy, adding another kilometre to the route. The cogwheel train now operates within the Budapest public-transportation network under tram line 60. You can use the usual public-transport tickets for this, or a travel pass if you have one.

When you leave the cogwheel railway, you'll find yourself near the top of Széchenyi-hegy.

SZÉCHENYI-HEGY

Széchenyi-hegy ❻ is actually on Svábhegy, and is one of the tallest hills in the group at 427 metres (1,400ft). It was once known as the Four Hills (Négy-hegy), but the name of Svábhegy arose from 'Swabian', a name for the group of people whose roots lie in south-west Germany, who had their artillery station here. After the death of István Széchenyi, a great politician whose name is also given to the Chain Bridge and the Széchenyi Baths, the highest part of the hill also received his name. It's a romantic part of the city, filled with lush villas and parkland, which became even more popular after the construction of the cogwheel railway.

It's also the point where the Children's Railway begins its 11km (6.8-mile) journey through the hills to Hűvösvölgy. From

Young worker on the Children's Railway

the cogwheel railway, head up Golfpálya út towards the top of the hill, where you'll find the station for the Children's Railway.

THE CHILDREN'S RAILWAY

The **Children's Railway** ❼ (Gyermekvasút; www.gyermekvasut.hu; seasonal times, see website) is a unique rail system that navigates the wooded Buda Hills. It is run entirely (engineers and drivers excepted) by children aged 10 to 14. From the ticket office to traffic control, you'll see diligent school children decked out in their train uniforms – often saluting on the platform as the train pulls in and out of the stations, or collecting tickets on board. Children are on duty on a voluntary basis (often every 15 days), and are given the day off school – should it fall on a weekday – providing the job doesn't affect their academic progress.

Buy your ticket at the station, then hop aboard this vintage old-timey train for an excursion into the Buda Hills. The concept of the Children's Railway originated in the USSR, with the first such railway opening in Gorky Park in Moscow. The aim was to encourage a positive work ethic among the youth in the Soviet Union and the other Red states. Under the communist regime, Hungary's Children's Railway was known as the Pioneer's Railway, named after the youth section of the Communist Party, changing its name in the 1990s after the fall of the Iron Curtain. The Children's Railway in Budapest opened in 1948, with the first line running from Széchenyi-hegy to Virágvölgy; the rest of the route was completed in 1950.

The route takes you through the woods and along the mountain ridge, stopping at a few stations, including Normafa. The track curves round the hills from Széchenyi-hegy to János-hegy and to Hárshegy.

The train ride takes about 45 minutes from Széchenyi-hegy to **Hűvösvölgy** ❽. At the final station, there's a little museum displaying items from the communist period.

Returning to the city from here is easy. Descend the stairs to the tram and hop on the 61 or the 56, both of which will take you back to Széll Kálmán tér.

Food and Drink

❶ BAJAI HALÁSZCSÁRDA

Hollós út 2; tel: 1 275 5245; http://bajaihalaszcsarda.hu; Tue–Sat 11.30am–10pm, Sun 11.30am–8pm in summer, until 6pm in winter, Mon closed; €€
This traditional Hungarian restaurant focuses on cuisine from the south of the country, most notably around Baja and Szeged, with its fresh-water fish dishes.

❷ SZAMOS SZÉPKILÁTÁS CUKRÁSZDA

Szépkilátás út 1; tel: 1 391 7740; https://szamos.hu; daily 9am–7pm; €
It's worth stopping here for its delightful conservatory. Get a selection of tasty cakes, coffees or savoury bites to fuel up on before heading back up into the hills.

DIRECTORY

Hand-picked hotels and restaurants to suit all budgets and tastes, organised by area, plus select nightlife listings, an alphabetical listing of practical information, a language guide and an overview of the best books and films to give you a flavour of the city.

Room with a view at the Hilton

ACCOMMODATION

Hotels in Hungary are graded from one to five stars. Budapest's standard visitor accommodation has improved dramatically in the years since the Iron Curtain came down. As well as a rise in quality, the number of places to stay has increased too, which for most of the year keeps prices at a very reasonable level. It is wise, however, to book ahead, particularly for September, New Year, Easter, at the turn of July and August, when the Hungarian Grand Prix is staged, and in mid-August, when the Sziget music festival is in full swing.

Hotel price depends on a variety of factors, such as the facilities available and location, with more central properties naturally being marked up at higher prices than suburban guest houses. The most popular areas include the Castle District and Pest's V District, as well as the inner parts of the VI, VII and VIII districts. If you opt for something further afield, the city's efficient public-transport system makes it easy to get around.

For cheaper accommodation, look into hostels and guest houses. Districts a little further out from the kernel of the city centre, such as the IX District, offer more affordable choices while still being easily accessible by public transport to the centre. Take note that some hostels in and around the Jewish Quarter are party hostels.

In the middle, you'll find standard and boutique hotels; the latter are best booked in advance as they tend to only have a handful of rooms and receive much interest.

When it comes to splurging, Budapest is rife with choice, from five-star hotels that come with their own spa or thermal bath to those set in beautiful, historic buildings with enviable views.

Castle Hill

Baltazár Budapest
Országház utca 31; tel: 1 300 7051; http://baltazarbudapest.com; €€€
A family-owned boutique hotel in the heart of the Old Town. Rooms have been individually designed and feature contemporary artwork and graphics juxtaposed with vintage furniture. Remarkably attentive staff. 11 rooms and suites.

Buda Castle Fashion Hotel
Úri utca 39; tel: 1 224 7900; www.mellowmoodhotels.com; €€€

Price for a double room in high season, including breakfast and VAT.
€€€€€ = over 250 euros
€€€€ = 200–250 euros
€€€ = 150–200 euros
€€ = 100–150 euros
€ = below 100 euros

Located in a 15th-century townhouse, this is a fully-equipped, modern, four-star hotel with 25 rooms. The interior design is classy and stylish. Major Buda sights are within walking distance.

Carlton Hotel

Apor Péter utca 3; tel: 1 224 0999; www.carltonhotel.hu; €€

The Carlton Hotel occupies a modern building at the foot of Fishermen's Bastion in a quiet alleyway. Four-stars, simply furnished and sparklingly clean. Some upper rooms have great views. Healthy buffet breakfasts. 95 rooms.

Hilton Budapest

Hess András tér 1–3; tel: 1 889 6600; www.hilton.com; €€€

One of the most famous hotels in town, occupying a plum location on top of Castle Hill. You'll either love or hate the modern hotel's incorporation of a 13th-century Dominican church. The excellent facilities include a business centre and babysitting service, and the Hilton's Icon restaurant has panoramic views of Fishermen's Bastion and Parliament. Wheelchair access. 322 rooms.

Lánchíd 19

Lánchíd utca 19; tel: 1 457 1200; www.lanchid19hotel.hu; €€

This bright and stylish boutique hotel occupies an enviable location just steps from the funicular up to the Castle District and the Chain Bridge across to Pest. The building is designed with glass panels arranged in waves on its façade, which change colour according to the season. Inside you'll find artworks by Françoise Gilot (one of Picasso's partners), designer furniture and sleek bathrooms. The three suites at the top of the building have Jacuzzi-baths with panoramic views of the city. 45 rooms and three suites.

St George Residence

Fortuna utca 4; tel: 1 393 5700; www.stgeorgehotel.hu; €€

Located in a reconstructed Baroque townhouse dating back to the 14th century and luxuriously refurbished, this hotel is full of exquisite charm. Rooms are elegant with stylish antique furnishings. There are standard, superior and executive suites available.

North Buda

Aquincum

Árpád Fejedelem útja 94; tel: 1 436 4100; www.aquincumhotel.com; €€

Located near the Árpád Bridge, Aquincum is a modern, luxury and refurbished thermal-bath hotel. Attractive restaurants and bars and an established executive club for business travellers. Wheelchair access. 310 rooms.

Hotel Császár

Frankel Leó út 35; tel: 1 336 2640; www.csaszarhotel.hu; €

For a Budapest spa break without breaking the bank, the Hotel Császár comes with unlimited pool access in the neighbouring Császár Komjádi

The colourful Aria Hotel

Swimming Pool Complex. You can also access the next-door Veli Bej Turkish baths with a discount of 20 percent – or, if you stay for three nights or more, you'll get a free ticket.

Central Pest

Aria Hotel Budapest
Hercegprímás utca 5; tel: 1 445 4055; www.ariahotelbudapest.com; €€€€€
Voted the world's number one hotel in 2017, this luxury boutique hotel comes with a unique design concept that merges music and architecture together. Its rooftop promises the best views in the city, overlooking St Stephen's Basilica. 49 rooms.

Budapest Marriott
Apáczai Csere János utca 4; tel: 1 486 5000; www.marriott.com/budhu; €€€€
A renovated city-centre hotel on the banks of the Danube. Every luxurious room enjoys splendid views of Castle Hill. Friendly, efficient service and excellent facilities, including business and fitness centres. Wheelchair access. 364 rooms.

Budapest Panorama Central
Károly Körút 10; tel: 1 328 0870; https://budapestpanoramacentral.com; €
The Panorama Central is a decent budget hotel in the centre of Pest, close to the Great Synagogue and other major sights, metro station and tram stops. Good value for money. 22 rooms split between two buildings.

Danubius Hotel Astoria
Kossuth Lajos utca 19–21; tel: 1 889-6000; www.danubiushotels.com; €€
The Astoria is like a film set. Opened in 1914, it comes with mirrors, chandeliers and carpets that evoke the ambience of the Belle Epoque. Café Astoria serves fine Hungarian fare. 138 rooms.

Four Seasons Hotel Gresham Palace Budapest
Széchenyi István tér 5–6; tel: 1 268 6000; www.fourseasons.com/budapest; €€€€€
Set in the stunning Gresham Palace with views over the Chain Bridge and the Danube, the Four Seasons Budapest offers true luxury with its elegant rooms and suites, as well as an on-site spa, fine dining and business facilities. 179 rooms.

Kempinski Hotel Corvinus
Erzsébet tér 7–8; tel: 1 429 3777; https://www.kempinski.com/en/budapest/hotel-corvinus; €€€€
The Kempinski inhabits an architecturally striking building and exhibits a great sense of style, elegance and flair. The hotel has its own 'Gastronomic Quarter', featuring the informal ÉS Bisztró and the modern Nobu restaurant, serving Japanese cuisine. Facilities include a business centre, swimming pool, fitness centre, shopping boutiques and even an art gallery. Wheelchair access. 351 rooms.

Ritz-Carlton Budapest
Erzsébet tér 9–10; tel: 1 429 5500; www.ritzcarlton.com; €€€€€

The former Adria Palace has been reborn as the Ritz-Carlton, with elegant rooms and suites, an on-site spa, the Deák Street Restaurant and the Kupola Lounge – all set under an Art Deco glass dome. Wheelchair access. 200 rooms and suites.

Sofitel Budapest Chain Bridge

Széchenyi István tér 2; tel: 1 266-1234; www.accorhotels.com; €€€€
The Sofitel is a luxury city-centre hotel with wonderful views over the Danube. There's a French-Hungarian gourmet restaurant, spa and sauna. The most striking feature is the atrium, which is an impressive eight floors high, decorated with palms, greenery and even a plane. The 357 rooms and suites are large and comfortable.

Starlight Suiten Hotel

Mérleg utca 6; tel: 1 484 3700; www. starlighthotels.com; €€
This stylish, mid-size, modern apartment hotel is ideally situated in the centre of town. Each suite contains everything you could need for a comfortable and hassle-free stay – from microwaves to cable televisions. There's also a sauna, fitness centre and café. 54 rooms.

Zenit Budapest Palace

Apaczai Csere János u. 7; tel: 1 799 8400; https://budapest.zenithoteles.com; €€€
This four-star hotel is located 50 metres from the Danube's river bank in the historical city centre. It was built in 1820 by the Hungarian architect Mihaly Pollack. Zenit has its own restaurant and even its own bakery. Here you can enjoy cookery demonstrations and a cocktail bar. 97 rooms.

The Jewish Quarter

Continental Hotel

Dohány utca 42; tel: 1 815 1000; http:// continentalhotelbudapest.com; €€€
Built on the site of the classic Hungária Spa, this four-star hotel blends Art Nouveau, Art Deco and modern design. There are 272 rooms and suites on offer.

Corinthia Hotel Budapest

Erzsébet krt. 43–9; tel: 1 479 4000; www. corinthia.com; €€€€€
Once the Grand Hotel Royal, the grandeur of fin-de-siècle Budapest, today's Corinthia blends elements of the old with the convenience of the new. You'll find a historic ballroom, a restored 19th-century spa and elegant restaurants. 414 rooms.

New York Palace Budapest

Erzsébet körüt 9–11; tel: 1 886 6111; www. dahotels.com/new-york-palace-budapest; €€€€
The hotel occupies one of the most beautiful buildings in the city, the New York Palace, designed in a flamboyant neo-Baroque style with ornate interiors and sumptuous fittings. Luxury, comfort and attention to detail are in abun-

Sofitel Budapest Chain Bridge pool

dance throughout. Facilities include a spa, cigar bar, business centre, restaurant and a café. 185 rooms.

ROOMbach
Rumbach Sebestyén utca 14; tel: 1 413 0253; https://roombach.com/en; €€
Located in the heart of the Jewish Quarter, ROOMbach mixes modern, colourful design with secure rooms that are ideal for the young, savvy traveller who wants to be at the heart of everything. 99 rooms.

Wombat's City Hostel
Király utca 20; tel: 1 883 5005; www.wombats-hostels.com; €
This clean and modern hostel on Király utca lies at the heart of the action. If you feel that dorm sharing isn't your thing, you can get private double or twin rooms at a budget price.

Andrássy Avenue

Mamaison Hotel Andrássy
Andrássy út 111; tel: 1 462 2100; www.mamaisonandrassy.com; €€
This four-star boutique hotel occupies a 1930s Bauhaus-inspired building by Alfréd Hajós, not far from Heroes' Square. The rooms are luxuriously appointed and some have four-poster beds. Guests at the Andrássy can also use the sauna and fitness centre of its sister hotel. 61 rooms and 7 suites.

Medosz Hotel
VI Jókai tér 9; tel: 1 374 3000; www.medoshotel.hu; €
A large hotel in the vicinity of Oktogon metro station. Rooms are not fancy, but are clean, comfortable and spacious. Some of them overlook Andrássy út. There's an excellent buffet breakfast.

Hotel Moments
Andrássy út 8; tel: 1 611 7000; http://hotelmomentsbudapest.hu; €€€
This elegant four-star hotel lies on Andrássy Avenue close to the Hungarian State Opera. It has its own lounge bar and house bistro offering a mix of Hungarian and international dishes. 99 rooms.

The Palace District

Brody House
Bródy Sándor utca 10; tel: 1 550 7363; www.brody.land; €€
This bohemian boutique hotel lies inside one of the original palaces in the district, where each of its rooms has been designed by a local artist. Guests get temporary membership to the affiliated Brody Studios member's club. 11 rooms.

Hotel Palazzo Zichy
Lőrinc Pap tér; tel: 1 235 4000; http://hotel-palazzo-zichy.hu; €€
Set in a 19th-century palace once belonging to Count Nándor Zichy and his family, this four-star hotel preserves the building's past with its historic

Mamaison Hotel Andrássy

façade. The rooms mix it up with contemporary design. 80 rooms.

Margaret Island

Ensana Grand Margaret Island

Margitsziget; tel: 1 889-4752; www.
ensanahotels.com; €€€
The Thermal Margaret Island's sister hotel is connected to its neighbour via an underground tunnel. The 'Grand Old Lady' of the island was built in 1893 in a neoclassical style. Guests can take advantage of its sister's facilities. 164 rooms.

Ensana Thermal Margaret Island

Margitsziget; tel: 1 889 4752; www.
ensanahotels.com; €€€
This hotel, built in 1979 in a Brutalist concrete style, was the city's first health resort. You'll find a fine spa, plus various therapies and health and beauty services on site, along with provisions for travellers with disabilities. 281 rooms.

South Pest

Corvin Hotel Budapest

Angyal utca 31–3; tel: 1 218 6566; http://
corvinhotelbudapest.hu; €€
Set between two wings, the Corvin and the Sissi, this may not be the most fashionable hotel in town, but it's clean, comfortable and close to the city centre, located in the heart of the renovated part of the IX District.

Ibis Budapest Centrum Hotel

Ráday utca 6; tel.: 1 456 4100; www.
accorhotels.com; €
This clean and comfortable central hotel has its own 24-hour bar and indoor parking. 126 rooms.

South Buda

Budapest art'otel

Bem rakpart 16–19; tel: 1 487 9487; www.
radissonhotels.com; €€€
This boutique hotel, styled by American contemporary artist Donald Sultan, displays 600 of his works. It is housed in four Baroque townhouses beside the Danube, opposite Parliament. It's a hip, lifestyle hotel with a good restaurant, the Chelsea, serving light, tasty meals. Wheelchair access. 165 rooms.

Danubius Hotel Gellért

Szent Gellért tér 1; tel: 1 889 5500; www.
danubiushotels.com; €€€
The famed Hotel Gellért faces the Liberty Bridge in Buda. Floodlit at night and visible across the city, it is a major architectural landmark, designed in exuberant Secessionist style. It has large rooms, antique furniture, splendid views and access to the facilities of the Gellért Baths. 234 rooms.

Hotel Victoria

Bem rakpart 11; tel: 1 457 8080; www.
victoria.hu; €€
This is a small, modern hotel facing the Danube on the Buda side. The rooms are spacious and the service is efficient and friendly. The price is excellent for the location. 27 rooms.

Enjoying a meal at Kéhli Vendéglő

RESTAURANTS

When it comes to eating out, there's plenty of choice in Budapest. From traditional Hungarian establishments – with white tablecloths and shakers of paprika instead of pepper – to modern restaurants, you'll find a variety of local dishes that sit side by side with international cuisine.

There's an eclectic mix up at Castle Hill and the surrounding areas. The folk art-adorned Hungarian restaurants are fun, but mainly cater to the tourist hoards, while trendy, contemporary restaurants put out updated dishes with a cosmopolitan edge.

In central Pest, around St Stephen's Basilica, the Parliament building and further out towards Kalvin tér, there are traditional restaurants, modern bistros and cuisines from all over the world. Pest is also home to most of the city's Michelin-starred restaurants, with Onyx (see page 45) and Costes (see page 102) leading the fine-dining scene.

It's best to avoid places that advertise in English (or another language besides Hungarian), as well as those that employ touts. If you're going to pay more for your meal, opt for somewhere that has a reputation for quality food instead. Of course, you'll find the usual international chains well represented if you're feeling a touch of homesickness.

Around lunchtime, keep an eye out for daily menu offers – you can usually get a cheap deal on 2–3 courses. Other budget options include street food, food trucks and eating at the food markets.

> Price guide for a two-course meal for one with a glass of house wine:
> €€€€ = over 60 euros
> €€€ = 40–60 euros
> €€ = 20–40 euros
> € = below 20 euros

Castle Hill

21 Magyar Vendéglő
Fortuna utca 21; tel: 1 202-2113; http://21restaurant.hu; daily noon–midnight; €€
This restaurant is resetting the standards by serving decent food at a fair price, and it well deserves its Michelin Bib Gourmand award. The cuisine here is solid Central European fare: Wiener schnitzel, roast duckling and pike perch.

Arány Kaviar
Ostrom utca 19; tel: 1 201 6737; http://aranykaviar.hu; Tue–Sun lunch noon–2.30pm, dinner 6–10.30pm; €€€
This hidden, romantic restaurant lies at the foot of the Royal Palace, specialising in Hungarian fish dishes and Russian caviar, fusing the two cuisines together in a fine-dining setting.

Kéhli Vendéglő dish

Csalogány 26

Csalogány utca 26; tel: 1 201 7892; www. csalogany26.hu; Tue–Wed noon–3pm, Thu–Sat noon–3pm and 9–10pm; €€

No-nonsense catering, with an emphasis on homely Hungarian cooking, makes this an excellent pit stop if you're in the Víziváros District after visiting Castle Hill. The reasonably priced set menu (lunchtime) ensures its popularity with local people.

Jamie's Italian Budapest

Szentháromság utca 9–11; tel: 1 800 9212; www.jamieoliver.com; daily 11.30am–11pm; €€€

Jamie Oliver may be an international name, but the first Jamie's Italian in Budapest is worth the visit, with terrace views over Matthias Church and Italian dishes with Jamie Oliver's signature twist added to them.

Pest-Buda Bistro

Fortuna utca 3; tel: 1 225 0377; www.pest-buda.com; Mon–Sun 7am–11pm; €€€

This bistro, set on the grounds of the Pest-Buda Hotel, offers traditional Hungarian dishes that have been updated without the clichés. Try the catfish *paprikash* with cottage-cheese noodles or the stuffed pepper, washed down with some Hungarian wine.

North Buda

Kéhli Vendéglő

Mókus utca 22; tel: 1 368 0613; www. kehli.hu; Mon–Fri noon–midnight, Sat–Sun noon–4pm and 5.30–11.30pm; €€

Kéhli is a family-owned tavern and one-time haunt of author Gyula Krúdy (1877–1933). The marrow-bone hot pot once relished by Krúdy is still on the menu, which also offers Hungarian and international cuisine. Finish your meal with a Hungarian trifle (*somlói galuska*).

Marxim

Kisrókus utca 23; tel: 1 316 0231; http://marxim.hu; Mon–Thu noon–1am, Fri–Sat noon–2am, Sun 6pm–1am; €

Workers of the world unite for communist-themed pizza served with panache. The menu shows considerable black humour, although Gulagpizza is said to be more nourishing than it sounds. The decor is propaganda of the past, the music is loud and the opening hours are long.

Nagyi Palacsintázója

Batthyány tér 5; www.nagyipali.hu; daily 24hours; €

A popular fast-food crêpe restaurant with several branches in the city (this one has nice views over the Parliament building), packed with locals and tourists alike. Delicious, good value for money and open round the clock.

Central Pest

Borkonyha Winekitchen

Sas utca 3; tel: 1 266 0835; http://borkonyha.hu; Mon–Sat noon–midnight, kitchen closed 4–6pm; €€€

Michelin-starred wine-oriented restaurant in the centre of Pest, offer-

Café Kör

ing the best of Hungarian cuisine with a contemporary touch. The name Winekitchen speaks for itself – the wine list is extensive and diverse, but most of them are Hungarian.

Café Kör

Sas utca 17; tel: 1 311 0053; Mon–Sat 10am–10pm; €€

Situated near Deák Ferenc tér, Café Kör has clean white tablecloths, friendly service and reasonable prices. It's popular so you'll need to book for peak times. Goose-liver pâté, spit roast, mixed grill, duck and some fine puddings ensure return visits. Cash only.

Cyrano

Kristóf tér 7–8; tel: 1 266-4747; http:// cyrano.hu; daily 8am–midnight; €€€

This chic restaurant is located right in the centre of town near Váci utca. The menu is French/Mediterranean inspired but with some traditional Hungarian touches. Inside, the ostentatious decor features the chandelier from the film set of *Cyrano De Bergerac*, starring Gérard Depardieu.

Fatál

Váci utca 67; tel: 1 266 2607; www. fatalrestaurant.com; daily noon–midnight; €€

The name might sound a bit dubious, but means 'wooden platter' in Hungarian. The platters here come heaped with Hungarian food, mostly quite meaty. The clientele are mainly tourists, but the food is good and the prices reasonable for Váci utca.

Kárpátia

Ferenciek tere 7–8; tel: 1 317 3596; www. karpatia.hu; Mon–Fri 11am–11pm, Sat–Sun 5–11pm; €€€

Built in 1877, Kárpátia is worth visiting for the decor alone, with its heavy gilding, stained glass and vaulted ceilings. The menu is based on Transylvanian and Hungarian cuisine, with goose, venison and Balaton pikeperch as options.

Kollázs Brasserie & Bar

Széchenyi István tér 5–6; tel: 1 268 5408; http://kollazs.hu; daily breakfast 6.30–10.30am, lunch noon–6pm, dinner 6–10.30pm, Sun brunch noon–3pm; €€€

Located within the elegant Four Seasons Hotel Gresham Palace, this elegant brasserie is headed up by Árpád Győrffy, the Bocuse d'Or Hungary award-winning chef. Try the French brioche or get adventurous with the 'Chef's Blind Date'.

Mátyás Pince

Március 15 tér 7; tel: 1 266 8008; www. matyaspince.eu; 11am–midnight; €€€

The Mátyás Pince serves traditional Hungarian dishes in an atmospheric turn-of-the-20th-century cellar setting. Anyone with a healthy appetite should try the King Mátyás platter. To round off the tourist's experience, there's gypsy music to ease your digestion.

Tom George Italiano

Október 6 utca 8; tel: 266-3525; www. tomgeorge.hu; Mon–Sun noon–midnight; €€

Lemon tart with strawberry compote

Tom George has a large, design-conscious interior and caters mainly to a young and lively crowd. The extensive menu offers international and Italian food, with the occasional nod towards Hungarian cuisine as well. There's a good cocktail menu, too.

Szimply

Károly krt 22; www.facebook.com/
szimplyfood; Mon–Sat 8am–4pm; €
Hidden inside the Röser udvar, Szimply serves up all-day breakfast with a twist. From classic avocado toasts to oatmeal, pancakes and specialty sandwiches, this is a tasty and healthy place for a chic brunch.

Zeller Bistro

Hercegprímás utca 18; tel: 30 651 0880;
www.zellerbistro.hu; Mon 8pm–midnight,
Tue–Sun noon–midnight; €€
This family-style farm-to-table restaurant offers homey flavours and interesting and innovative recipes. The menu is seasonal and changes on a monthly basis. Try the elderflower champagne, deer steak and amazing carrot cake. Booking is a must.

The Jewish Quarter

Bors Gastrobar

Kazinczy utca 10; tel: 70 935 3263; https://
www.facebook.com/BorsGasztroBar; daily
11.30am–9pm; €
For cheap eats with a gourmet twist, Bors Gastrobar comes with excellent soup and sandwich combinations, care-fully prepared with quality ingredients. The menu changes regularly. Be prepared to queue!

Kőleves Vendéglő

Kazinczy utca 41; tel: 1 322 1011; https://
kolevesvendeglo.hu; Mon–Wed 8am–11pm,
Thu and Fri 8am–midnight, Sat 9am–
midnight, Sun 9am–11pm; €€
This bright and unpretentious restaurant in the Jewish Quarter offers classic Hungarian-Jewish cuisine as well as a range of excellent vegetarian dishes. In the summer, there's a charming garden bar open next to the restaurant.

La Bodeguita del Medio

Kertész utca 36; tel: 20 388 2738; www.
labodeguitadelmedio.hu; Sun–Thu
noon–1am, Fri–Sat noon–3am; €€
Located in a pretty, charmingly dilapidated garden courtyard in the city's old artists' club, this restaurant serves Cuban and Latin American dishes. A live Cuban band plays every evening, with dance shows on Saturday nights.

Mazel Tov

Akácfa utca 47; tel: 70 626 4280; www.
mazeltov.hu; Sun–Wed 10am–1am, Thu–Fri
10am–2am; €€
This Jewish-themed restaurant captures the ruin-bar look, but with more chic than shabby aesthetic. You'll find dishes ranging from grilled meat to hummus and *shakshuka* on the menu, along with tasty salads. Good wine and *pálinka* range.

Chic Costes

Paneer

Király utca 53; tel: 30 336 9060; www. paneer.hu; Sun–Wed 11am–11pm, Thu 11am–1am, Fri–Sat 11am–2am; €

This cheese bar is a must for cheese lovers. While technically a street food place, this branch of Paneer is a restaurant, where you can sit upstairs or on the benches downstairs. Come here for fried-cheese burgers, great pasta dishes with a cheesy twist or a modern take on the classic Hungarian fried cheese.

Andrássy Avenue

Bigfish Seafood Bistro

Andrássy út 44; tel: 1 269 0693; www. thebigfish.hu; daily noon–10pm; €€

At Bigfish, diners can choose from a selection of fish/seafood to be prepared by the chef. It may feel like eating in a market at times, but the place is a must for fish lovers.

Drop Glutenfree Restaurant

Hajós utca 27; tel: 1 235 0468; http:// droprestaurant.com; Mon–Sun noon–11pm (kitchen closes at 10pm); €€

Drop offers a tasty range of gluten and lactose-free dishes, as well as vegetarian options.

Komédiás Kávéház

Nagymező utca 26; tel: 1 302 0901; www. komediaskavehaz.hu/en; Mon–Fri 10am–midnight, Sat–Sun 1pm–midnight; €€

This Belle Epoque-themed café and restaurant captures the spirit of the Hungarian operetta, with portraits of famous singers adorning the walls. The food is a mix of traditional Hungarian, Jewish and French. Live piano music after 7pm (Wed–Sun).

Kozmosz

Hunyadi tér 11; tel: 20 514 6663; http:// vegankozmosz.hu; Mon–Fri 11.30am–3pm and 6–10pm, Sat–Sun 11.30am–10pm; €€

This vegan restaurant, tucked into a basement on Hunyadi tér, offers dishes including traditional Hungarian classics recreated using plant-based alternatives. Not just a healthy-eating place, Kozmosz creates food that is diverse, delicious and appealing to non-vegans, too.

Pesti Disznó

Nagymező utca 19; tel: 1 951 4061; www. pestidiszno.hu; €€

Pesti Disznó reworks traditional Hungarian flavours and ingredients into bite-sized portions, kind of like a Hungarian tapas bar – or bite bar, as they call themselves. Try their reinvented sausages, bean stews and stuffed cabbage.

South Pest

Costes

Ráday utca 4; tel: 1 219 0696; www.costes. hu; Wed–Sun 6.30–11pm; €€€€

This Michelin-starred restaurant presents refined international dishes, which sometimes draw on the robust flavours of Hungarian cuisine for inspiration. Alongside meat and fish-orien-

Budapest serves up some refined plates

tated showpieces, seasonal dishes dot the menu. Smart casual dress code.

Esetleg Bar & Bistro

Fővám tér 11–2; tel: 70 413 8761; www. facebook.com/pg/esetlegbar; €€

Located at the entrance to the Bálna complex, Esetleg has a splendid terrace overlooking Liberty Bridge and Gellért Hill in the distance. The food here mixes up Hungarian dishes with your usual bistro fare, and the design is industrial-chic.

Petrus

Ferenc tér 2–3; tel: 1 951 2597; www. petrusrestaurant.hu; Tue–Sat noon–3.30pm and 6.30–11pm; €€€

Combining French bistro cuisine with Hungarian home cooking, Petrus evokes grandmother's kitchen with a modern, gourmet accent and seasonal flair. Try the tasting menu if you're in the mood to spoil yourself.

Vörös Postakocsi

Ráday utca 15; tel: 1 217 6756; www. vorospk.com; daily 11am–midnight; €€

If you're looking for authentic Hungarian cuisine with all the trimmings, then Vörös Postakocsi has got you covered, complete with the folk art and the gypsy band.

South Buda

Hemingway

Kosztolányi Dezső tér 2; tel: 30 488 6000; http://hemingway-etterem.hu; Mon–Sat noon–midnight, Sun noon–4pm; €€€

The proprietor is an Ernest Hemingway fan, and the decor evokes the writer's world. The menu is seasonal and includes, of course, swordfish.

Veganlove

Bartók Béla út 9; www.veganlove.hu; Mon–Sun 11am–9pm; €

A great place for anyone interested in trying some tasty vegan street food. You'll find a selection of vegan burgers, such as the sweet-potato burger and BBQ tofu burger. Other vegan delights on offer include their special hot-dog recipe.

Buda Hills

Larus

Csörsz utca 18/BB; tel: 1 799 2480; https:// larusetterem.hu/en; €€€

Located next to the MOM Cultural Center, this restaurant offers an interesting fusion of French and Hungarian cuisine. You can enjoy your dinner in an airy and stylish dining room or during the summer dine on the outdoor terrace.

Náncsi Néni Vendéglője

Ördögárok utca 80; tel: 1 397 2742; www. nancsineni.hu; daily noon–11pm; €€

A traditional restaurant with paprika dangling from the ceiling and gingham cloths and fresh bread on the tables. Auntie Néni's home cooking is rustic Hungarian fare and it comes in large helpings. Located close to the Children's Railway.

Bartók Béla National Concert Hall at the Palace of Arts

NIGHTLIFE

There is something for everyone in Budapest, whether you're looking to attend a classical concert among gold-gilded halls or drink beer in a crumbling ruin bar. Budapest is a city where events take place on a nightly basis, and if there is no concrete programme, you can pop into one of the hundreds of watering holes in the city.

For shows, you can buy tickets online from the venue website or simply pop into the box office. Tickets for theatre, opera, ballet and classical concerts are more reasonably priced in Budapest than in many other cities, perhaps because Hungarians don't see the arts as highbrow and elitist.

Most of the city's venues are relaxed, so there is no need to dress up to the nines unless you want to, although it doesn't hurt to don something smart for the opera. From classical music to jazz clubs and gritty ruin pubs, keeping yourself entertained is never difficult in Budapest.

Classical music, theatre and ballet

Bartók Béla National Concert Hall
Komor Marcell utca 1; tel: 1 555 3000; www.mupa.hu
This 1596-seat (plus 60 standing places) concert hall lies inside the Palace of Arts complex. One of the best concert halls in Europe, it stages concerts and recitals featuring the biggest names in classical and contemporary music.

Erkel Theatre
II János Pál pápa tér 30; tel: 1 332 6150; www.opera.hu
The sister theatre to the Hungarian State Opera, the Erkel Theatre (Erkel Színház) is one of Budapest's more modern theatres, and is also the largest when it comes to musical theatre and opera. You'll find affiliated productions with the State Opera being performed here in a more contemporary setting, and with the benefit of wheelchair access.

Hungarian State Opera House
Andrássy út 22; tel: 1 814 7100; www.opera.hu
A landmark in its own right, this beautiful opera house is the heart of the classical music scene in Budapest. It is the finest of the city's opera venues and connoisseurs rank it among Europe's best. Seasons usually run from September to June, with top-billed opera, ballet and musical productions. The opera house is currently undergoing renovation. While this is underway, performances are being shown at the Erkel Theatre.

Liszt Ferenc Academy of Music
Liszt Ferenc tér 8; tel: 1 462 4600; http://zeneakademia.hu/en/home, https://lfze.hu

Housing the world-famous music academy, this building is also home to the Liszt Academy Concert Center, which delivers programmes of the very highest quality featuring performances from some of the world's best musicians and orchestras. The splendid Art Nouveau music hall was built in 1904, and it's worth visiting for the architecture alone.

The National Theatre
Bajor Gizi park 1; tel: 1 476 6800; https://nemzetiszinhaz.hu

The National Theatre occupies an avant-garde building that combines modern architectural elements with classical ones. The theatre building incorporates 21,000 sq metres (226,000 sq ft), making it the largest theatre in Budapest. The programme focuses on classic theatre, mainly in Hungarian.

Trafó House of Contemporary Arts
Liliom utca 41; tel.: 1 215 1600; http://trafo.hu

For avant-garde theatre and dance, Trafó offers an alternative experience to mainstream and classical theatre. You can see a variety of productions here, including circus, modern dance and even puppet theatre.

Vigadó Concert Hall
Vigadó tér 2; tel: 20 429 4124; http://vigado.hu

With names like Liszt, Brahms, Debussy and Bartók having per-formed here, the Vigadó has a fine pedigree when it comes to classical music. The venue, which is home to Budapest's second-largest concert hall, holds theatre productions and concerts, such as the Hungarian Gala Concert.

Music venues

A38
Petőfi híd budai hídfő; tel: 1 464 3940; www.a38.hu

This repurposed Ukrainian stone-carrying ship has become one of the most popular concert venues and bars in the city. It's easy to spot the boat – it's permanently moored under the bridge on the Buda side of the river. Programmes include pop, rock, alternative, jazz, electro and even experimental acts.

Akvárium Klub
Erzsébet tér 12; tel: 30 860 3368; http://akvariumklub.hu

Located in the heart of the city, this subterranean venue gets its name from its transparent glass roof that contains a large pond above. Akvárium is a cultural centre that holds a variety of events, from mainstream concerts to underground acts and local bands. There are two large concert halls, as well as a few bar areas. In the summer, the terrace is a popular hangout for Budapest's young crowd.

Budapest Jazz Club
Hollán Ernő utca 7; tel: 1 798 7289; www.

bjc.hu

For quality jazz and blues acts, Budapest Jazz Club has got you covered, with nightly live-music acts from home and abroad. The interior captures the Art Deco grandeur of the jazz age, and if you're hungry or thirsty, there is also a café in the front of the venue.

Budapest Park

Soroksári út 60; tel: 1 434 7800; www.budapestpark.hu

This location stands as Budapest's largest open-air concert venue, stretching for more than 11,000 sq metres (118,400 sq ft). This seasonal venue brands itself as a permanent festival site, holding top-billed concerts and events from April to October, making it one of the hottest spots for music in the summer months.

Ruins bars and nightlife

Anker't

Paulay Ede utca 33; tel: 30 360 3389; www.facebook.com/pg/ankertbar

Hidden behind the door to a block of gutted apartments, Anker't is one of the largest ruin bars in the city. While predominantly an outdoor venue, in the winter a tent covers the main bar area. You'll find DJ nights, large international parties and various events held in this minimalist ruin pub.

Boutiq'Bar

Paulay Ede utca 5; tel: 30 554 2323; www.boutiqbar.hu

A favourite with mixologists, if you like cocktails than you can't go wrong with this gourmet cocktail bar. While the bartenders can shake up or stir your favourite cocktail into shape, you can also try some more unusual concoctions with a seasonal twist, or ingredients like Caribbean rose peppercorn.

Corvin Club & Roof Terrace

Blaha Lujza tér 1–2; tel: 20 244 7230

For an underground atmosphere above the city, the Corvin Club occupies the rooftop of a Social Realist department store. In the summer, its roof terrace is a popular spot for parties and film nights, whereas its club is a hive of DJs and electronica icons from Hungary and the rest of Europe. Expect the party to continue until dawn.

Csendes Vintage Bar & Café

Ferenczy István u. 5; tel: 30 727 2100; https://www.csend.es

Popular downtown ruin bar. This place features diverse and unique decor – unique statues, graffiti and quirky furniture – strangely all of this together somehow creates a nice and cosy atmosphere.

Doboz

Klauzál utca 10; tel: 20 449 4801; http://doboz.co.hu

This ruin bar-meets-club is a party hotspot in the heart of the Jewish Quarter. While its interior is derelict, it's a little

more refined than other ruin bars, featuring themed spaces and work by contemporary Hungarian artists, as well as parties that go on until 6am.

Ellató Kert

Kazinczy utca 48; tel: 20 527 3018

Hidden in a courtyard on Kazinczy utca, this popular watering hole captures the original ruin-bar feeling in its simplicity – even with its Mexican-themed decor and taco stand. Ellató Kert is one of the few ruin bars in the VII District where you'll find locals on a night out.

Instant-Fogas

Akácfa utca 49–51; tel: 30 123 4567; https://instant-fogas.com

After Szimpla Kert, Fogas Ház and Instant were the largest ruin bars in Budapest. When Instant closed its original venue on Nagymező utca in 2017, its installations moved to a new location, joining forces with Fogas Ház to create a ruin-bar party complex on Akácfa utca. You'll also find other bars, like Liebling and techno club LÄRM, on the premises for the ultimate night out in Budapest.

Morrison's 2

Szent István krt 11; tel: 1 374 3329; www.morrisons2.hu

Boasting six dance floors, a wide range of musical sounds and even karaoke, Morrison's is a significant contender for being the biggest club in the city. This is a venue for all-nighters, catering mostly to the university crowd. You'll find a variety of drinks and cocktails on offer, and even food should you get peckish.

Ötkert

Zrínyi utca 4; tel: 70 330 8652; http://otkert.hu

You'll find this club and cultural venue close to St Stephen's Basilica. Hosting exhibitions, concerts and happening parties for Budapest's trend setters, Ötkert is a popular spot for locals and tourists alike, centred around a beautiful courtyard.

Szatyor Bár

Bartók Béla út 36; tel: 1 279 02 91; www.szatyorbar.com

This gallery is filled with eclectic and colourful designs. Szatyor offers delicious food (a fusion of domestic and international cuisine) and rich cultural art programs. During the summer, there is a lovely outdoor seating space.

Szimpla Kert

Kazinczy utca 14; tel: 1 352 4198; www.szimpla.hu

The first and original ruin bar, no trip to Budapest would be complete without stepping into the wonderland that is Szimpla Kert. Built up over a network of rooms belonging to an old apartment block, Szimpla is decked out with surreal art and repurposed furniture. On Friday and Saturday nights, expect the place to be packed.

Kozponti Antikvarium, the largest antique bookshop in Eastern Europe

A–Z

A

Age restrictions

The legal age to drink alcohol in Hungary is 18; the same when it comes to buying cigarettes and other tobacco products. While it is legal to drive a car at 17, most car-rental companies only allow drivers aged 21 and above (age may vary depending on the category) to hire their vehicles (drivers under 25 may incur a young-driver surcharge).

Airport

The **Budapest Liszt Ferenc International Airport** (BUD; formerly Budapest Ferihegy; tel: 1 269-7000; www.bud. hu) is around 16km (10 miles) from the city centre. Terminal 2A serves flights in the Schengen zone and Terminal 2B serves all non-Schengen destinations (until 2012 there used to be a Terminal 1, hence the names 2A and 2B). Both terminals are connected by the Sky-Court, a state-of-the art passenger hall. The airport has car-hire desks, bureaux de change, ATM machines and information offices, and the Wi-Fi internet is available free of charge. There is an observation terrace at the Terminal 2A departure hall.

It takes about 30 minutes to get from the airport to the centre of Budapest. The efficient **MiniBud Airport Shuttle Service** (tel: 1 550 0000; www.mini-bud.hu) is the best deal; it is a shared taxi that will deliver you to and collect you from any address in Budapest. A one-person single fare from the airport to the city centre can cost from HUF 1900 (€6). Look for the prominent 'MiniBud Shuttle Bus' sign at the information desk. For the return journey, call 24 hours in advance to book. Your hotel will do this for you. There is also a **public airport bus**, No. 200E (BKK; www.bkk. hu). This is much cheaper (a one-way ticket is HUF 350, and HUF 450 when bought from the driver), and deposits passengers at the Kőbánya-Kispest metro station. There is also a new bus route 100E, that stops in Kálvin tér, Astoria and Deák tér (HUF 900 a ticket).

B

Budgeting

The currency in Hungary is the Hungarian forint (HUF; see page 115) – make sure to check the exchange rate before you travel, or download an app to calculate costs as you go. Visitors expecting the dirt-cheap Central Europe of the past may be in for a shock, as shops and many restaurants charge the same as Western European countries. One thing that does remain very inexpensive, however, is the highly efficient public-transport system.

Budapest's Children's Railway

Generally, a regular beer will cost you HUF 500–600 (approximately €2), whereas a glass of house wine will set you back HUF 500–900 (up to €3). A main course at a budget restaurant costs around HUF 2,000 (around €6), a moderately priced restaurant will see mains priced between HUF 3,000 and 6,000 (€10–20), with mains going above HUF 6,000 in a top gourmet restaurant. You can find a cheap hotel room for around HUF 9,000–18,000 (€30–60), but in general, a double room with taxes and breakfast will cost HUF 30,000–45,000 (€100–150), with luxury hotels going above HUF 75,000 (€250) a night.

A taxi from the airport to the city centre could easily cost between HUF 6,600 and 10,000 (around €20–35), depending on the exchange rate and distance. When it comes to public transport, a single-ride ticket (metro, tram, bus) will cost around HUF 350 (€1.15), a 24-hour ticket HUF 1,650 (just over €5), and a 72-hour ticket HUF 10,900 (about €35).

You can also opt for the **Budapest Card** (Budapest Kártya; www.budapest-card.com), which allows the holder 24, 48 or 72 hours' travel and sightseeing. A booklet comes with the card, detailing all the services available. These include free travel on public transport; free admission to museums and baths; free walking tours; and discounts at restaurants, shops, on tickets for cultural programmes and many other attractions. The card costs €21.99 (roughly HUF 7,000) for 24 hours, €32.99 (around HUF 11,000) for 48 hours and €42.99 (approximately HUF 14,400) for 72 hours. It is available online, at the airport, Budapest tourist information points, hotels and main metro stations.

Children

With its large zoo, outdoor spaces and child-friendly restaurants, Budapest is a good place for kids. You'll find a number of playgrounds scattered around the city's public spaces to keep the little ones entertained. Museums and monuments come with a children's discount. Popular spots for families with kids include Margaret Island, the Budapest Zoo and Botanical Garden and the Children's Railway.

Clothing

Dress is indistinguishable from that in any other European capital. Dress smartly in casinos and more upmarket restaurants.

Crime and safety

Budapest has a low rate of violent crime, but use your common sense, don't take risks and be wary of pickpockets. Watch your belongings, especially on public transport or in crowded places. It's wise to make photocopies of travel documents and keep them in a separate place, such as a hotel safe.

Theft should be reported to the police – there are plenty of police stations in the

Traditional dolls for sale

city. Remember to get a copy of your statement for your own insurance purposes. The emergency services phone number is 112. There is also a 24-hour hotline in English to report crime (tel: 1 438 8080).

Customs

Most visitors require a valid passport to enter Hungary. Since joining the EU, citizens of other European Union countries require only an ID card. Citizens of many non-European countries do not need visas either. The Ministry of Foreign Affairs maintains a helpful and up-to-the minute website reporting requirements and changes (http://konzuliszolgalat.kormany.hu). Those who need visas may obtain them from the Hungarian consulate in their country of residence. There are single, double- and multiple-entrance visas.

The Hungarian National Tax and Customs Administration (NTCA) also maintains a website (www.nav.gov.hu) giving details of regulations. Travellers, from outside of the European Union, may bring 200 cigarettes, a litre of spirits (more than 22 percent alcohol by volume) and two litres of wine or other alcoholic beverages (containing less than 22 percent alcohol by volume). However, there are no restrictions to the amount of alcohol and cigarettes visitors travelling from another European Union country may bring, provided the goods are all for personal use, and not for sale. There are no currency restrictions, although leaving or entering the EU with large amounts of cash – €10,000 or more – should be declared.

Value-added tax, or VAT (known as ÁFA in Hungary), can be reclaimed on goods costing more than HUF 50,000 (by non-EU residents only). Shops participating in the scheme are responsible for making the refund to travellers who are entitled to it.

Driving

To take your car into Hungary you need a valid driving licence and car-registration papers. Cars from most European countries are presumed to be fully insured, so no extra documentation needs to be shown. However, Central Budapest boulevards are many lanes wide and you have to contend with trams and trolley buses as well as heavy traffic.

Electricity

The current is 230 volts throughout Hungary. Take a two-pin adapter as necessary.

Embassies and consulates

Australia: enquires should be directed to the Australian embassy in Austria, Mattiellistrasse 2–4, Vienna; tel: +43 1 506740; www.austria.embassy.gov.au
Canada: Ganz utca 16; tel: 1 392 3360; www.canadainternational.gc.ca/hungary-hongrie

Andrássy Avenue

Ireland: Szabadság tér 7 (in Bank Centre); tel: 1 301 4960; www.dfa.ie/irish-embassy/hungary
UK: Füge utca 5–7; tel: 1 266 2888; www.gov.uk/government/world/organisations/british-embassy-budapest
USA: Szabadság tér 12; tel: 1 475 4400; https://hu.usembassy.gov

Etiquette

In general, Hungarians are polite people. A young person will greet their elders with '*csókolom*', which means 'I kiss it', a throwback to the time when hands were kissed. '*Jó napot kívanok*', meaning good day, is more commonly used when greeting shop owners and service people, whereas the younger, more familiar crowd will say '*szia*' or the Westernised 'hello' instead (sometimes hello is even used to say goodbye). When greeting each other, younger people usually do the European two kisses on the cheek when familiar with each other, but the standard handshake is also acceptable when first meeting or in more formal settings. When one is invited into a Hungarian's home, bring a gift such as a bunch of flowers or a bottle of wine.

F

Festivals

January
Budapest International Circus Festival
Taking place every two years, this five-day festival showcases circus artists and performers from numerous countries.
https://www.fnc.hu/eng/festival

February
Mangalica Festival
This gastronomic event is all about Hungary's curly-haired Mangalica pig. Taste a variety of products made from this unique Hungarian heritage breed.
http://mangalicafesztival.hu
Budapest Dance Festival
This annual festival held at the National Dance Theatre features a range of dance, from ballet to contemporary dance and even folk dance.
http://budapesttancfesztival.hu

March
March 15
A national holiday in Hungary to commemorate the Hungarian Revolution of 1848 and independence from Habsburg rule. A number of events take place across Budapest, including concerts and speeches.

April
Budapest Spring Festival
This city-wide cultural festival brings the best in classical music, opera and jazz to the city, with more than 50 performances held across Budapest's most important venues.
https://btf.hu/index.php
Titanic International Film Festival
This is the largest international film festival in Hungary, showcasing films from

Revellers at Sziget Festival

over 20 countries, including international premiers.
http://titanicfilmfest.hu

Budapest100
Go behind the scenes in Budapest during this architecture festival. Each year, there is a different theme, from buildings that are 100 years old to Danube-side buildings, allowing you to take a peek into some splendid structures that are usually closed to the public.
http://budapest100.hu

May

Rosalia Rosé Festival
Learn all about Hungarian rosé wines, as well as sparkling wines. There are tastings, concerts and more.
https://rosalia.hu

Budai Gourmet Festival
Try the best in local gastronomy with food featured by Budapest's top restaurants, local winemakers and *pálinka* distillers.
https://gourmetfesztival.hu/hu

July

Budapest Pride
The week-long Budapest Pride Film and Cultural Festival features film screenings, theatre performances, talks, concerts and parties, and of course, the Pride Parade.
http://budapestpride.hu

Formula 1 Hungarian Grand Prix
The famous Hungarian Grand Prix takes place at the Hungaroring Grand Prix Circuit in Mogyoród each summer (late July early August).
http://hungaroring.hu

August

Sziget Festival
For a week in August, one of Europe's biggest festivals, Sziget, takes over the majority of Óbuda Island, with concerts from top-billed artists, local and international bands and a variety of installations, parties, bars and more.
https://szigetfestival.com/en

St Stephen's Day
August 20th marks a national holiday to celebrate King István and his creation of the Hungarian state. You'll find a number of events around the city, particularly near the Royal Palace, which culminate in a spectacular firework display above the Danube.

September

Budapest Short Film Festival
Towards the end of August and the beginning of September, Budapest becomes the epicentre of the short-film world with its showcase of short films from young and developing filmmakers around the world. The event is held in English with English subtitles.
https://busho.hu/hu

Jewish Summer Festival
This festival comes with the goal of introducing Jewish Culture to as many people as possible. The event features music, dance, fine art and film screenings, hosted at the Great Synagogue and around the Jewish Quarter.
www.zsidokulturalisfesztival.hu

Budapest Wine Festival
Held on the grounds of the Royal Pal-

ace, with views over the Danube, the Budapest Wine Festival features the country's top winemakers along with folk music and gourmet bites.
www.aborfesztival.hu

October
Budapest Design Week
Usually beginning at the end of September and running into October, Budapest Design Week showcases just why Budapest earnt its nickname, the 'City of Design'.
www.designweek.hu
October 23
This national holiday remembers the Hungarian Uprising against the Soviet Army in 1956. It's a sombre day, with memorials and events taking place across the city.
Art Market Budapest
A large exhibition and art fair aiming to raise the profile of contemporary artists from Central and Eastern Europe.
http://artmarketbudapest.hu

November–December
Budapest Christmas Market
From November till the beginning of January, the Budapest Christmas Market is in full swing, with stalls featuring Hungarian designers and local, seasonal gastronomy.

H

Health
Hungarian doctors and health-care professionals are highly skilled, and most speak English and German. The Hungarian National Health Service is well equipped to handle emergencies and there are reciprocal arrangements for citizens of the EEA (European Economic Area), which includes the EU member countries plus Norway, Iceland and Liechtenstein. Emergency treatment is free for foreigners; all other treatment has to be paid for when you receive the service. EU residents should obtain the European Health Insurance Card, which entitles them to medical and hospital treatment free of charge. Please check for new regulations post-Brexit.

The American **FirstMed Center** is located in Buda (Hattyú utca 14; tel: 1 224-9090; http://firstmedcenters. com). For 24-hour medical care, call **Swiss Clinic** (Váci út 30; tel: 30 992 0387; www.swissclinic.hu), which has an ambulance service.

Tap water is drinkable, but don't drink anything marked *nem ivóviz*, which means non-drinkable.

Pharmacies. Look for the sign *gyógyszertár* or *patika*. Chemists only sell pharmaceutical and related products. For cosmetics and toiletries you will need an *illatszer bolt* or *drogéria*. The Tourinform offices carry lists of pharmacies. One of the night pharmacies is **Teréz Patika** (VI Teréz körút 41; tel: 1 311 4439; www.terezpatika.hu).

Hours and holidays
Most businesses in Budapest are open Mon–Fri 8am–5pm. **Shopping cen-**

Mai Manó House of Hungarian Photography

tres are open Mon–Sat 10am–9pm, Sun 10am–7pm. Smaller **shops** are open Mon–Fri 9 or 10am–6 or 7pm, Sat 9 or 10am–1 or 2pm, but some close all day Saturday. For 24-hour shopping look for the sign 'Non-Stop'. **Banks** open Mon–Fri 8am–4 or 5pm, although some close at 3pm on Friday. **Museums** mostly open Tue–Sun 10am–6pm. **Post offices** open Mon–Fri 8am–6pm, Sat 8am–1pm.

1 January New Year's Day
15 March National Holiday Anniversary of 1848 Revolution
April Good Friday
April Easter Monday
1 May Labour Day
June Pentecost
20 August St Stephen's Day
23 October Remembrance (Republic) Day
25 December Christmas Day
26 December Second Day of Christmas

Internet facilities

Hotels, shopping centres, restaurants and cafés offer free Wi-Fi access, which is also available at the airport and on some squares. See www.wificafespots.com for a map of the city's Wi-Fi access spots. There are also several internet cafés. Vist@NetCafe (Váci út 6; tel: 70 585 3924; www.vistanetcafe.com) in the very centre of the city is open 7am–midnight, and you can also scan and print your documents there.

Language

Hungarian is the mother tongue of 95 percent of the population. It is wholly unrelated to the languages of the surrounding countries and is classified in the Finno-Ugric family of languages. It is notoriously difficult and continues to baffle linguists. Many Budapestis speak German, and many, especially the young, speak English fluently.

One source of confusion is how to address a Hungarian. The surname always precedes the Christian name; Western Europeans would say or write Károly Jókai, whereas Hungarians say Jókai Károly. Second, there is no direct equivalent of Mr or Mrs; the nearest terms, which are very formal, are *Uram* for Mr and *Hölgyem* for Mrs. You can mix East and West by saying, for example, Mr Jókai.

LGBTQ travellers

The LGBTQ community in Budapest is still not wholly accepted by the mainstream population. However, the age of consent for gay sex in Hungary is now 14, the same as for heterosexuals. The main support organisation for the LGBTQ community is called **Háttér** (tel: 329-2670; www.hatter.hu). **CoXx Men's Bar** (VIII Dohány utca 38; www.coxx.hu) is a popular gay venue in Budapest. Budapest has a pretty active gay community.

Newspapers and magazines can be bought at city newsstands

M

Media

Newspapers and magazines. *Budapest Business Journal* (https://bbj.hu) is the English-language weekly newspaper in the city. Major European and US newspapers usually arrive on the day of publication, although some are a day late. *Pesti Est* (http://est.hu) has comprehensive listings of nightlife activities along with *Funzine* (http://funzine.hu).

Television. All hotels rated four star and above, and some three star, offer satellite television.

Money

Currency. The unit of currency is the forint (HUF). Coins in circulation are HUF 5, 10, 20, 50, 100 and 200. Banknotes are in denominations of HUF 500, 1,000, 2,000, 5,000, 10,000 and 20,000.

Foreign exchange offices. These are found in banks, hotels, larger campsites, travel agents and large shops, but some offer exchange rates as much as 20 percent lower than banks, which always offer the most advantageous rates. There isn't a black market anymore, so if you are accosted and offered money-changing opportunities, steer clear. It's good to have a few dollars, euros or pounds for emergencies, and you may get a better rate of exchange for cash.

Credit and debit cards. Visa, MasterCard and AmEx are frequently accepted in hotels, restaurants and large shops (look for the logos). Smaller shops, some museums and railway stations expect payment in cash. Post offices (there are more than 3,200 of them) will dispense cash on production of your card.

ATMs. Cash machines are widespread and most major cards are accepted. They dispense HUFs. However, there are also two ATMs in the centre of Budapest that dispense euros: in Deák Ferenc utca 5–7 and Babér utca 9.

Taxes. All hotels and restaurants charge an 18 percent VAT rate, although this should be included in the price. Sometimes it is added separately, however. There is also a 4 percent city tax which should be included in your hotel rate, but some add it on top of the price – ask the hotel before booking if taxes are included in the price.

P

Post

Post offices (Magyar Posta) handle all mail. Stamps (*bélyeg*) are best bought at tobacconists or where postcards are sold. Most hotels will stamp and post your mail for you. Post boxes are painted red.

Most post offices open Mon–Fri 8am–8pm, Sat 8am–4pm. The office near station Nyugati (Teréz körút

51–53) opens 7am–8pm and the one near Keleti Sation (Baross tér 11/c) is open at all hours.

Religion

The majority of Hungarians are Roman Catholics. Mass is usually said in Hungarian, but in some churches it is said in Latin, English or German. Other denominations and faiths, notably Protestant, Eastern Orthodox and Jewish, are also represented. There is a small Muslim community.

S

Smoking

While there are a high number of smokers living in Budapest, indoor public spaces are non-smoking, and smoking has been restricted around playgrounds, underpasses and even in public-transport stops. Tobacco has been limited to state-controlled, yet privately owned, National Tobacco Shops (Nemzeti Dohánybolt).

Telephones

You can roam on one of three Hungarian mobile networks or buy a local SIM card. The mobile network operators are: Magyar Telekom (www.telekom.hu), Telenor (www.telenor.hu) and Vodafone (www.vodafone.hu).

To make an international call from a public phone, dial the international access code (00), followed by the country code and the telephone number, including the area code. There are no off-peak rates. For national calls beyond Budapest, dial the national access code (06), followed by the area code and number. A local call within Budapest has 7 digits; it is not necessary to dial the area code. Mobile telephone numbers have 9 digits. The network is being modernised, so numbers change frequently. If the number has changed, there's a message in Hungarian followed by one in English (so don't hang up) giving the new number. For international directory assistance, tel: 199.

Dialling codes:

Hungary (Budapest): +36 (1)
Australia: +61
Canada: +1
Ireland: +353
UK: +44
USA: +1

Time zones

Hungary follows Central European Time (Greenwich Mean Time +1 hour, or US Eastern Standard Time +6 hours). In summer the clock is put one hour ahead (GMT +2), meaning when it's noon in Budapest it's 11am in London and in New York it's 6am.

Tipping

Tipping is the norm in Hungary. It is customary to leave 10 percent at

Waiter at a Budapest restaurant

restaurants and round up the bill in bars. Some restaurants may add a 10 or 12.5 percent service charge to the bill, so look carefully and ask, if this appears to be the case, so that you avoid tipping twice. Porters, hotel maids, toilet attendants, folk violinists playing at your table, masseurs at thermal baths and tourist guides also expect tips.

Toilets

In Budapest public toilets are usually pay toilets. A lot of restaurants and cafés require a code to use the bathroom (this is typically found on the receipt). Some bars will have a toilet attendant who'll give you toilet paper for a few coins. The cleanest toilets are usually found in shopping malls.

For men's toilets, look out for the word *Férfiak* or, more commonly, *férfi* (occasionally *urak*). For women, look for *Nők* or (again, more commonly) *női* (and occasionally *hólgyek*).

Tourist information

The **Tourism Office of Budapest** operates tourist information points at Deák Ferenc Square, Sütő utca 2; Budavár (Holy Trinity square pavilion), Tárnok u. 15; Heroes' Square, Olof Palme sétány 5; and it has branches at both terminals of the Budapest Airport (www.budapestinfo.hu and http://tourinform.hu). A **tourist information hotline** is maintained on tel: 1 438-8080 (Mon–Fri 8am–8pm).

IBUSZ (http://ibusz.hu) is a major tour operator, providing a booking service and organises excursions.

There is a **Hungarian National Tourist** Office in the UK (46 Eaton Place, London SW1 X8AL; Mon–Thu 9am–5pm, Fri 9am–3pm; tel: (020) 7823-0413; https://hellohungary.com/en).

Tours and guides

There are numerous guided tours available in Budapest: **Cityrama** (tel: 302-4382; www.cityrama.hu); **Budatours** (tel: 374-7072; http://budatours.hu); **Program Centrum** (tel: 317-7767; www.programcentrum.com) and **IBUSZ** (tel: 485-2750; http://ibusz.hu) offer a range of services.

Tours are available to the Danube Bend, the Puszta, and Lake Balaton; as are special-interest tours (health and wellness, seasonal customs and folklore, etc.).

Mahart Passnave (tel: 484-4013; www.mahartpassnave.hu) and **Legenda LTD** (tel: 317-2203; https://legenda.hu/en) are perhaps the most established operators offering Danube boat trips. The shortest of the cruises are hour-long sightseeing tours with commentary in various languages. In the summer, day trips are available, taking passengers up the Danube Bend to the historic towns of Esztergom, Szentendre and Visegrád. There are also evening cruises with buffet suppers, music and dancing.

Riding the tram

You can also go sightseeing in Budapest by helicopter, light aircraft or hot-air balloon. Hotel reception areas have brochures about excursions and Tourinform can also help.

Budapestbike.hu (tel: 30 944-5533; http://budapestbike.hu) organises guided bicycle tours, including an evening one that takes in Budapest's better nightspots. The company provides men's, women's and tandem bikes, along with helmets and other accessories.

Yellow Zebra Segways & Bike Tours (tel: 269-3843; www.yellowzebratours.com) are organised daily all year-round (check website for details).

Transport

The **Budapest Transport Authority** (BKK) operates an extensive system with four metro lines, blue local buses, yellow trams and red trolley-buses. You must buy a ticket before boarding. They are sold at stations, travel bureaux and tobacconists. If you are staying for several days, it makes sense to buy a three- or seven-day travel card. Current fares and additional information are available at www.bkk.hu.

Most public transport runs between 4.30am and 11.30pm. There are a limited number of night buses and trams (night buses have a number in the 900s). Don't forget to validate your ticket by punching it in the red or yellow machine (passes don't need validating), which are located aboard buses and trams, and at the entrance to metro stations. BKK ticket inspectors, wearing purple armbands and sometimes in uniform, but most often in plain clothes, patrol public transport frequently and levy fare dodgers with on-the-spot fines.

Buses *(busz)*. A bus stop is marked by a blue-bordered rectangular sign with the letter M and a list of stops on the route.

Trams *(villamos)*. Yellow trams, usually of three to four carriages, cover a 190km (120-mile) network; some run throughout the night.

Taxis *(taxi)*. Budapest's taxi drivers are notorious for overcharging foreigners, and unless you're laden with luggage or have some other reason for not travelling on public transport, they should be avoided. If, however, you do want a taxi, call one of the following firms: **Citytaxi** (tel: 1 211 1111; www.citytaxi.hu), **Fő Taxi** (tel: 1 222 2222; www.fotaxi.hu), or **Taxi4** (tel: 1 444 4444; www.taxi4.hu). Hailing a cab on the street is not recommended, but if you do so, always find out the rate and make sure the meter is working (and set at zero before you set off), or agree on the fare in advance. You can also use an app like **Bolt** (https://bolt.eu).

Metro. The only interchange between the metro's three lines used to be at Deák tér station. However, a fourth line of the Budapest metro opened and another interchange stop is at Kálvin tér or at Keleti Pályudvar. Metro 4 has 10 stations so far and

The Budapest metro

runs under the Danube, connecting the southwestern Kelenföld railway station (Kelenföldi vasútállomás) in Buda, and the eastern Keleti Railway station (Keleti pályaudvar) in Pest. The single fare costs HUF 350, and HUF 450 when bought aboard. If you need to change lines in order to get to your destination, buy a transfer ticket (HUF 530). There is also a 24-hour travel card (HUF 1,650).

Trains. There are four HÉV suburban commuter lines: to Szentendre, Gödöllö (with a branch line to Csömör), Csepel and Ráckeve. Szentendre (via Aquincum) is reached via Batthyány tér station and Gödöllö is reached from Örs vezér tere. If you have a travel card, you pay only for the stretch outside Budapest city limits. Intercity trains operate from three Budapest stations: **Keleti** (Baross tér; most international trains), **Nyugati** (Nyugati tér; mostly destinations east) and **Déli** (Alkotás út).

The main **railway ticket office** for national and international trains is located at Andrássy út 15 (Máv-Group; tel: 349-4949; www.mavc soport.hu/en).

A special treat for train enthusiasts are the **nostalgia trains**, vintage and steam locomotives run by Máv Nosztalgia (ticket office at Teréz krt. 55; tel: 269-5242; www.mavnosztalgia.hu) that go to the Gödöllö Palace, the Hungarian Plain, Danube Bend and Eger. The *Royal Hungarian Express* visits

the cities of the old Austro-Hungarian Empire (Prague and Vienna).

River transport. In the summer season the Budapest Transport Authority operates a boat service between Rómaifürdö, Batthyány tér, Szent Gellért tér, Haller utca and the National Theatre. Pleasure boats run to and from the Danube Bend; hydrofoils also run to Esztergom and Vienna (Mahart Pass Nave; tel: 484-4013; www.mahart passnave.hu).

Travellers with disabilities

Budapest is busy improving access for travellers with disabilities. Currently, access ranges from excellent to non-existent. Public transport is difficult, but there are now buses and some trams equipped to take wheelchairs on certain routes. The metro line 4 also offers full disabled access. Furthermore, there is a door-to-door taxi service using special minibuses with hydraulic lifts that can be called upon (BKK; www.bkk.hu; tel: 70 390 3414) on weekdays between 5.30am and 11.30pm and weekends between 8am and 4pm.

A few additional metro stations have lifts, and more are planned. Some museums are accessible. The spa hotels are fully equipped, and many larger hotels have some adapted rooms and wheelchair access. Some hotels located in old villas and palaces may not have disabled access – enquire at the hotel before booking.

City signpost

LANGUAGE

Even the most linguistically confident of non-Hungarian speakers is likely to feel daunted when attempting to get by in Hungarian. A Finno-Ugric language – related to Finnish and Estonian among others – with an alphabet of 44 characters, Hungarian is notoriously difficult to learn, and local people will not expect you to have mastered it before you visit. Any efforts you make will be readily appreciated, however. The following list is a selection of useful words and phrases to get you started.

General

Hello *Szervusz/Szia* (informal)
Goodbye/Bye *Viszontlátásra/Viszlát*
Yes/No *Igen/Nem*
Please *Kérem (szépen)*
Thank you *Köszönöm*
Excuse me *Elnézést*
Sorry *Bocsánat*
Please speak slowly *Tessék lassabban beszélni*
I don't speak Hungarian *Nem beszélek magyarul*
Do you speak English? *Beszél angolul?*
Can you help me? *Kérhetem a segítségét?*
My name is... *A nevem...*
Is there... here? *Van itt...?*
Where is...? *Hol van...?*
Railway station *Pályaudvar*
Airport *Repülőtér*
Ticket office *Jegypénztár*

Entrance/exit *Bejárat/kijárat*
Push/pull *Tolni/húzni*
Left/right *Bal/jobb*
Straight on *Egyenesen*

Numbers

Zero *Nulla*
One *Egy*
Two *Kettő, két*
Three *Három*
Four *Négy*
Five *Öt*
Six *Hat*
Seven *Hét*
Eight *Nyolc*
Nine *Kilenc*
Ten *Tíz*
One hundred *Száz*
One thousand *Ezer*

Days of the week

Monday *Hétfő*
Tuesday *Kedd*
Wednesday *Szerda*
Thursday *Csütörtök*
Friday *Péntek*
Saturday *Szombat*
Sunday *Vasárnap*

Time

What time is it? *Hány óra van?*
It is 1 o'clock *Egy óra van*
It is 2 o'clock *Két óra van*
Now *Most*
Today *Ma*

Poem ('One Sentence on Tyranny' by Gyula Illyés) inscribed on the main gates to Memento Park

Tomorrow Holnap
Yesterday Tegnap
Early morning Reggel
Mid/late morning Délelőtt
Afternoon Délután
Evening Este
Open/closed Nyitva/zárva

Emergencies

Help! Segítség!
Stop! Stop!
Police Rendőrség
Doctor Orvos
Ambulance Mentőautó
Hospital Kórház

Shopping

How much is this? Ez mennyibe kerül?
I'm just looking Csak körülnézek
Do you accept credit cards? Fizethetek kártyával?
Market Piac
Pharmacy Patika
Post office Postahivatal
Supermarket Bevásárlóközpont

Eating out

May I have the menu, please? Kérek egy étlapot?
I'd like... Kérnék...
Waiter/Waitress Pincér/Kisasszony
Bon appétit! Jó étvágyat!
I'm a vegetarian Vegetáriánus vagyok
Where is the toilet? Hol van a WC?
Gents/Ladies Férfi/Női
The bill, please Számlát kérek
Is service included? Ebben a felszolgálás is benne van?

Beef Marhahús
Beer Sör
Bread Kenyeret
Butter Vajat
Chips Hasábburgonya
Coffee Kávé
Duck Kacsa
Fish Hal
Goose Liba
Lamb Bárány
Milk Tej
Pepper (seasoning) Borsot
Pepper (vegetable) Paprika
Pork Sertéshús
Potato Burgonya
Rabbit Nyúl
Red wine/white wine Vörös bor/Fehér bor
Rice Rizs
Salt Só
Sparkling wine Pezsgő
Sugar Cukor
Veal Borjú
Water/mineral water Víz/Ásványvíz

Internet and social media

What's the Wi-Fi password? Mi a Wifi jelszó?
Are you on Facebook/Twitter? Van Facebook-od/Twitter-ed?
What's your username? Mi a felhasználóneved?
I'll add you as a friend Hozzáadlak barátnak
I'll follow you on Twitter Követni foglak Twitteren
I'll tag you in the pictures Bejelöllek a képen (tag)

BOOKS AND FILM

In recent years, Hungarian literature has exploded in popularity, with writers such as Imre Kertész (winner of the Nobel Prize), Laszló Krasznahorkai (winner of the Man Booker), Péter Eszterházy, Magda Szabó and Péter Nádas. However, Hungary has a rich literary history, made up of iconic poets like József Attila and Sándor Petőfi and writers like Ferenc Molnár and Ferenc Móra. Hungarian literature has frequently captured the mood of its time – with important literary depictions of the Habsburg Empire, the Holocaust, communist Hungary and beyond.

When it comes to cinema, Budapest is no stranger to film shoots, and has stood in as a location double for Paris, Argentina, Moscow and even New York. The city has featured in numerous films, including Midsommar (2019), *Blade Runner 2049* (2017), *The Martian* (2015), *Evita* (1996) and *Munich* (2005).

Hungarian cinema itself is rich and thought-provoking, with László Nemes' *Son of Saul* (2015) winning both an Academy Award and a Golden Globe for Best Foreign Language Film. Hungarian films often evoke a vivid combination of the surreal and absurd juxtaposed against stark realism. Some address contemporary issues – several older films even critiqued the communist regime, like banned black comedy *The Witness* (1969). Hungarian film-making hasn't shied away from avant-garde storytelling either, as seen in Hungary's first Oscar-winning film, *Mephisto* (1981), or any of Béla Tarr's works.

Books

Non-fiction
A Guest in My Own Country by György Konrád. This powerful memoir captures the turbulent history of Budapest in the mid-20th century. After fleeing the countryside for Budapest just a day before Jewish deportations reached his home town, Konrád captures his life and struggles in the city, from the Siege of Budapest to the Hungarian Uprising of 1956.

Budapest 1900 by John Lukacs. This book, about Budapest at the height of its golden age (the late 19th–early 20th century), offers a scholarly, yet accessible, cultural study of the city at its prime.

Budapest: A Critical Guide by András Török. While technically a guidebook, Török looks at local culture and history in further depth.

Hungarian Wine by Robert Smyth. Learn all about Hungary's wines, from grape types and wine regions to which Hungarian wines you should be drinking.

The Food and Wine Lover's Guide to Hungary by Carolyn Bánfalvi. For the gastronomically inclined, Bánfalvi's book offers an introduction to Hungarian cuisine, along with restaurant tips and a handy guide to the best places to eat and drink in Budapest.

Angry dogs in White God

Fiction

Colours and Years by Margit Kaffka. Margit Kaffka's novel is considered one of the great works of 20th-century Hungarian fiction for its richly developed characters. It has a strong autobiographical element, being based on her mother's life, and explores the societal constraints imposed on women at the time.

Fatelessness by Imre Kertész. A semi-autobiographical story by Nobel Prize-winner Imre Kertész, about a 14-year-old Jewish boy living in Budapest who is sent to Auschwitz. The boy manages to survive the Holocaust, and returns home, trying to readjust to life in his home city.

The Paul Street Boys by Ferenc Molnár. This book, written in 1907, captures life in the VIII District in the early 20th century. A piece of classic youth literature, Molnár weaves an exciting plot peppered with colourful characters.

The Door by Magda Szabó. Poignant and beautifully written, this character-based novel set in Budapest focuses on a young writer and her eccentric, mysterious housecleaner, Emerence. A moving and harrowing story.

The Baron's Sons by Mór Jókai. Jókai's novel takes place during the events of the Hungarian Revolution and the War of Independence (from the Habsburgs) in 1848–9. It centres around the Baradlay family and those acquainted with them, painting a colourful depiction of Hungry and the revolution.

Under the Frog by Tibor Fischer. A Man Booker Prize finalist, this novel chronicles the adventures of two Hungarian basketball players during the period between the end of World War II and the Hungarian Uprising of 1956.

Film

Kontroll (2003). A surreal film looking at the life of ticket inspectors on the metro. Filmed entirely in Budapest's underground network at night, this stylish film offers a mix of action, black humour and a surreal twist.

Son of Saul (2015). Set in Auschwitz, *Son of Saul* follows Saul Ausländer, a Hungarian-Jew who is a member of the *Sonderkommando*. The film has won countless awards, including an Oscar.

The Witness (1969). This classic black comedy by Péter Bacsó was banned for more than a decade for its depiction of the Hungarian communist regime.

White God (2013). Kornél Mundruczó's film is set in a world where owners of mixed-breed dogs must pay outrageous fines. When Lili is separated from her dog, Hagen, a chain of events escalates when 250 dogs follow Hagen on a rampage through the city. *White God* was Hungary's entry for the 87th Academy Awards.

On Body and Soul (2017). This drama film, written and directed by Ildikó Enyedi, won the Golden Bear at the 67th Berlin International Film Festival and was nominated for the Best Foreign Language Film Oscar at the 90th Academy Awards. A love story between two people who work together and share the same dream every night.

ABOUT THIS BOOK

This *Explore Guide* has been produced by the editors of Insight Guides, whose books have set the standard for visual travel guides since 1970. With top-quality photography and authoritative recommendations, these guidebooks bring you the very best routes and itineraries in the world's most exciting destinations.

BEST ROUTES

The routes in the book provide something to suit all budgets, tastes and trip lengths. As well as covering the destination's many classic attractions, the itineraries track lesser-known sights, and there are also excursions for those who want to extend their visit outside the city. The routes embrace a range of interests, so whether you are an art fan, a gourmet, a history buff or have kids to entertain, you will find an option to suit.

We recommend reading the whole of a route before setting out. This should help you to familiarise yourself with it and enable you to plan where to stop for refreshments – options are shown in the 'Food and Drink' box at the end of each tour.

For our pick of the tours by theme, consult Recommended Routes for… (see pages 6–7).

INTRODUCTION

The routes are set in context by this introductory section, giving an overview of the destination to set the scene, plus background information on food and drink, shopping and more, while a succinct history timeline highlights the key events over the centuries.

DIRECTORY

Also supporting the routes is a Directory chapter, with a clearly organised A–Z of practical information, our pick of where to stay while you are there and select restaurant listings; these eateries complement the more low-key cafés and restaurants that feature within the routes and are intended to offer a wider choice for evening dining. Also included here are some nightlife listings, plus a handy language guide and our recommendations for books and films about the destination.

ABOUT THE AUTHORS

Jennifer Walker is an ex-physicist turned travel writer, with a focus on Budapest and the surrounding regions. She comes from a mixed background of British and Hungarian heritage and grew up between East Sussex and Budapest – she returned to live in the Hungarian capital in 2013.

CONTACT THE EDITORS

We hope you find this Explore Guide useful, interesting and a pleasure to read. If you have any questions or feedback on the text, pictures or maps, please do let us know. If you have noticed any errors or outdated facts, or have suggestions for places to include on the routes, we would be delighted to hear from you. Please drop us an email at hello@insightguides.com. Thanks!

CREDITS

Explore Budapest
Editor: Zara Sekhavati
Author: Jennifer Walker
Head of DTP and Pre-Press: Rebeka Davies
Update Production: Apa Digital
Managing Editor: Carine Tracanelli
Picture Editor: Tom Smyth
Layout: Aga Bylica
Cartography: updated by Carte
Photo credits: Adrienn Szabo/Bonfire/
Cafe Film/Kobal/REX/Shutterstock 122;
Alamy 36, 52, 53, 64, 65, 80, 86/87, 123;
Balazs Mohai/Epa/REX/Shutterstock 25;
Four Seasons 90MC, 95; Getty Images
22, 24, 26, 27, 28/29T, 30/31, 70/71,
76/77, 90/91T, 105, 106; Hilton 92; iStock
10, 11, 14/15T, 40T, 73, 74/75, 112,
113; Leonardo 96; Library Hotel Collection
90MC, 90MR, 90ML, 94; Ming Tang-Evans/
Apa Publications 4ML, 4MC, 4MR, 4MR,
4MC, 4ML, 6TL, 6MC, 6ML, 6BC, 7MR, 7M,
7MR, 8ML, 8MC, 8ML, 8MC, 8MR, 8MR,
12, 12/13, 13L, 14B, 16, 16/17, 17L, 18,
19, 20, 20/21, 21L, 22/23, 28ML, 28MC,
28MR, 28ML, 28MC, 28MR, 32, 32/33,
33L, 34, 34/35, 35L, 38, 38/39, 39L,
40/41, 41L, 42, 43, 46, 46/47, 47L, 48,
49, 55, 56, 56/57, 57L, 58, 58/59, 59L,
60, 60/61, 61L, 62/63, 63L, 66B, 66/67,
67L, 72, 74, 75L, 76, 77L, 78, 82, 82/83,
83L, 84, 84/85, 85L, 89, 90ML, 90MR, 93,
97, 98, 99, 100, 101, 102, 103, 104, 107,
108, 109, 110, 111, 114, 115, 116, 117,
118, 119, 120, 121; Richard Sowersby/
REX/Shutterstock 37; Shutterstock 1, 4/5T,
7T, 8/9T, 23L, 40B, 44, 45, 50, 51, 54, 62,
66T, 68, 69, 81, 88; SuperStock 79
Cover credits: Shutterstock (all)

Printed in China by RR Donnelley

Second Edition 2020

DISTRIBUTION

UK, Ireland and Europe
Apa Publications (UK) Ltd
sales@insightguides.com
United States and Canada
Ingram Publisher Services
ips@ingramcontent.com
Australia and New Zealand
Woodslane
info@woodslane.com.au
Southeast Asia
Apa Publications (Singapore) Pte
singaporeoffice@insightguides.com
Worldwide
Apa Publications (UK) Ltd
sales@insightguides.com

SPECIAL SALES, CONTENT LICENSING AND COPUBLISHING

Insight Guides can be purchased in bulk
quantities at discounted prices. We can
create special editions, personalised jackets
and corporate imprints tailored to your needs.
sales@insightguides.com
www.insightguides.biz

INDEX